PRAISE FOR *DESTINED FOR THE CROSS*

"Dr. Randy Clark is the wi_____ _____ newest book, *Destined for the Cross*, is a brill_____ th and resurrection. I can't imagine readi_____ nsformation in how you view the nature _____ ly appreciate everything that happened at the cross, we must understand both the enormity of Christ's sacrifice and how eternity was forever changed at Calvary. Read this book, and let each chapter reveal a new facet of the unfathomable gift of grace revealed in the cross. As God's intentional love for humanity unfolds through these pages, let it evoke new waves of gratitude, turning our hearts to our Savior. We owe Him nothing less than absolute surrender through our *yes*!"

—BILL JOHNSON, SENIOR LEADER OF BETHEL CHURCH, REDDING,
    CALIFORNIA; AUTHOR OF *THE WAY OF LIFE* AND *RAISING GIANT-KILLERS*

"When Randy Clark speaks, I listen. His vital experience of the Christian faith has helped so many to find healing, restoration, and hope in Jesus."

—ERIC METAXAS, #1 *NEW YORK TIMES* BESTSELLING AUTHOR OF *BONHOEFFER*,
    MARTIN LUTHER, AND *MIRACLES*; HOST OF THE *ERIC METAXAS RADIO SHOW*

"*Destined for the Cross* is an instant Christian classic about the most precious subject in Christianity that every people group and denomination share a passion for: the cross of Christ. Both theologically brilliant but simple and relevant, Randy Clark brings together a book on the cross that will be a final word on the subject to you, your friends, family, and coworkers. If someone asks you about why Jesus had to die, and what the cross is all about, I promise you will borrow language from Randy's book. . . . It is just that kind of powerful tool that might just be the before and after you personally needed with who Jesus is and why He chose to die for you!"

—SHAWN BOLZ, AUTHOR OF *TRANSLATING GOD*, *BREAKTHROUGH*, AND *THROUGH THE
    EYES OF LOVE*; HOST OF *EXPLORING THE PROPHETIC* AND TBN'S *TRANSLATING GOD*

"*Destined for the Cross* is one of the greatest works ever to be written on the cross of Jesus Christ. This good news is not only about what we have been saved *from* but also reveals what we are saved *to*. You will be inspired to live the true gospel and the whole gospel after reading this book."

—LEIF HETLAND, PRESIDENT OF GLOBAL MISSION
    AWARENESS; AUTHOR OF *CALLED TO REIGN*

"Dr. Randy Clark is one of my favorite teachers. His childlike wonder at the beauty of Jesus combined with comprehensive theological knowledge is rare and beautiful. This excellent book, *Destined for the Cross*, combines wisdom and research with deep love for Jesus, the only One who is worthy. Let the words on these pages stir your hunger to walk as Jesus did and experience all He promised us. May your love for Him and your understanding of His powerful love for you overflow more every single day."

—HEIDI G. BAKER, PHD, COFOUNDER AND EXECUTIVE
    CHAIRMAN OF THE BOARD FOR IRIS GLOBAL

"Randy is an evangelist wonderfully used by God throughout the world in recent decades. His passion for Jesus Christ and for his readers is that they might experience a complete gospel, a full salvation (spirit, soul, and body), effectively communicated in every page of this book. The book is profoundly *kerygmatic*, making it possible for any reader who is seeking God to clearly perceive that Jesus died on the cross because of His love for us, so that we might experience fullness of life, liberty, healing, forgiveness, and eternal life. That is to say that we might live according to God's original plan."

—CARLOS MRAIDA, PHD, SENIOR PASTOR AT CENTRAL CHURCH OF BUENOS
    AIRES, THE OLDEST AND SECOND LARGEST BAPTIST CHURCH IN ARGENTINA

"In this book, Randy Clark majors on the major matters: who Jesus is and why He died for us. Throughout eternity, we'll explore ever more deeply the meaning of God's love for us and hatred of evil revealed in the cross. Randy invites us to begin that contemplation now."

—CRAIG KEENER, PHD, PROFESSOR OF BIBLICAL STUDIES
    AT ASBURY THEOLOGICAL SEMINARY; AUTHOR OF
    CHRISTOBIOGRAPHY AND *NOT AFRAID OF THE ANTICHRIST*

"If you want to know the significant difference the cross of Christ has for your life, this is the book for you. Randy Clark masterfully weaves sixteen different reasons Christ was crucified with personal stories and testimonies from almost fifty years of ministry experience. Each story makes these sixteen reasons come alive in a way that will stir your heart to increased faith. It certainly did that for me. Good theology should make a practical difference and this book does just that!"

—DR. SCOTT MCDERMOTT, PHD IN NEW TESTAMENT STUDIES; LEAD
    PASTOR OF THE CROSSING UNITED METHODIST CHURCH

"From one of this century's most influential leaders in the global Pentecostal-Charismatic movement comes this crossover book. Integrating biblical interpretation with personal anecdotes, *Destined for the Cross* should be read not only by Pentecostals and Charismatics, but also by evangelicals, liberals, and Roman Catholics."
—CANDY GUNTER BROWN, PhD, PROFESSOR OF
    RELIGIOUS STUDIES AT INDIANA UNIVERSITY

"The depths of what the Cross has accomplished often get overlooked or neglected in a popular Christian culture that prefers sound bites to sound theology. The outworking of our salvation is cross-shaped. To follow Jesus is to live a cruciform life. Randy Clark takes us on a journey into the depths of the Father's love, revealed through the Person and Work of His Beloved Son at the Cross. His theological expertise and his astute insight will serve this generation and emerging generations well with a sweeping overview of the utter comprehensiveness of not only the Cross of Christ, rather also how the apostles preached it. This work is timely and much needed."
—BISHOP MARK J. CHIRONNA, MA, DMIN

"In a day when increasing numbers of people both outside and inside the church have such a limited understanding of why Jesus died, Dr. Clark shines light on the eternal truth of the world-changing event of the cross."
—DR. TOM LITTEER, DMIN, ASSISTANT DEAN AND ADJUNCT
    PROFESSOR AT GLOBAL AWAKENING THEOLOGICAL SEMINARY

"Recognized internationally as a revivalist and evangelist, Randy Clark is also an astute theologian. His insights are marked by Spirit and truth—brandished on the front lines of global missions. *Destined for the Cross* is watershed work, positioning believers to reenvision the beauty and wonder of Jesus. Clark reminds us in this transitional hour that everything hinges on the cross of Christ."
—J. D. KING, PASTOR AT WORLD REVIVAL CHURCH; ACADEMIC
    DEAN AT REVIVAL TRAINING CENTER; AUTHOR OF *REGENERATION:
    A COMPLETE HISTORY OF HEALING IN THE CHRISTIAN CHURCH*

"If you have read Randy's many other books on healing, you will find *Destined for the Cross* takes you to a whole new level. Randy goes through the reasons Jesus had to die in the first few chapters, issues much debated by theologians. . . . You need to read this summary of all the practical wisdom God has taught Randy through his many years of ministry. Although He would not seek a comparison to Thomas Aquinas, I believe this is Randy's *Summa Theologica*."
—STEPHEN MORY, MD, PSYCHIATRIST AND RESEARCHER

"As the world plunges into a morass of fear, doubt, and confusion engendered by the COVID-19 pandemic, one fact remains paramount. That Jesus died on the cross and rose again. His power alone can rescue a world in chaos, a world without hope, a people that have lost their way. With fresh revelation Randy Clark examines the meaning, the significance, and the eternal legacy of Christ's death on the cross. His approach is informed, scholarly, and is illustrated by powerful contemporary examples of God's intervention in the lives of people. I recommend it without reservation."

—DR. ERNEST FRANK CROCKER, BSc(MED), CONSULTANT
    PHYSICIAN IN NUCLEAR MEDICINE; AUTHOR OF *NINE*
    MINUTES PAST MIDNIGHT AND *WHEN OCEANS ROAR*

"There is nothing as precious as the blood that was shed for us. Dr. Clark's book is a powerful call to all those in the Lord's service to gather united and humbled at the foot of the cross. A very timely word!"

—NEAL LOZANO, FOUNDER OF HEART OF THE FATHER MINISTRIES;
    AUTHOR OF *UNBOUND: A PRACTICAL GUIDE TO DELIVERANCE*

"This is a remarkable work! Dr. Randy Clark has a gift both spiritually and biblically that draws us, the reader, into the accomplishments of the redemption and sufferings of Christ."

—DR. BRUNO LERULLO, DMIN, MMIN, MTS, BA; AUTHOR OF *UNITED IN CHRIST*

"Truly the message of the cross is as relevant and powerful today as it was two thousand years ago. For those who assume that Jesus' passion is irrelevant or even nonsensical, Randy Clark responds with fresh, clear, and credible explanations from Scripture, reinforced by moving personal testimonies. A perfect book to give to seekers who are thirsty for God."

—MARY HEALY, PROFESSOR OF SACRED SCRIPTURE; AUTHOR OF *MEN AND WOMEN*
    ARE FROM EDEN AND *HEALING: BRINGING THE GIFT OF GOD'S MERCY TO THE WORLD*

DESTINED
FOR THE CROSS

16 REASONS JESUS HAD TO DIE

RANDY CLARK

EMANATE
BOOKS

Published in Nashville, Tennessee, by Emanate Books, an imprint of Thomas Nelson. Emanate Books and Thomas Nelson are registered trademarks of HarperCollins Christian Publishing, Inc.

Thomas Nelson titles may be purchased in bulk for educational, business, fund-raising, or sales promotional use. For information, please e-mail SpecialMarkets@ThomasNelson.com.

Any Internet addresses, phone numbers, or company or product information printed in this book are offered as a resource and are not intended in any way to be or to imply an endorsement by Thomas Nelson, nor does Thomas Nelson vouch for the existence, content, or services of these sites, phone numbers, companies, or products beyond the life of this book.

ISBN 978-0-7852-2428-0 (TP)
ISBN 978-0-7852-2429-7 (eBook)

Library of Congress Control Number: 2020934396

Printed in the United States of America

20 21 22 23 24   LSC   10 9 8 7 6 5 4 3 2 1

I dedicate this book to the most important people on earth to me—my wife, DeAnne; my adult children and their spouses, Josh and Tonya, David and Johannah Leach, Josiah and Allie, and Jeremiah and Lizzie; and my grandchildren, Simeon, Selah, Malakai, Nova, Ember, Ronan, Harper, and Juliet. I want each of you to know the profound benefit of Jesus' death for you.

CONTENTS

FOREWORD

by David F. Watson

The message of the cross sounded like foolishness in the first century, just as it does to many today. In the twenty-first century we are no less sinful than we were in the first. Our culture is one of selfies, social media, and self-aggrandizement. The message of the cross—a message of self-denial and sacrificial love—will sound strange, even offensive. In North America we have for decades tried to make the Church "attractional" in the hopes that people would find us appealing enough to keep attending each week. The tailwinds of cultural Christianity in the West, however, have faded away. The solution is not to continue trying to become enough like the culture to remain attractive. We cannot do that without sacrificing the core of the gospel. The solution is to accept the offense of the message of the cross and rely once again upon the power of God to demonstrate the truth of our proclamation.

Some would call this "power evangelism." I would simply call it biblical Christianity. On page after page of the Bible we read of a God who is ever-present, who is actively involved in the affairs of human life. This God is not an absentee landlord but a Father, a King, a Savior who seeks the well-being of His children. It was this same God who became flesh in Jesus Christ, who died an atoning death on the cross, and after three days rose from the dead. The Lord of all creation died on a Roman cross, and, to paraphrase the late Richard John Neuhaus, that cross became the axis upon which all of creation turns.

Dr. Randy Clark, who has taught us for so many years about miracles, has now given us a gift in this book about the miracle of the cross. I consider Randy one of the most important voices in the Christian world today. He consistently points us back to the God of our Bible, a God who moves with power, a God who heals and speaks and saves. Randy will not allow us to rest content with God as an idea, a God who simply provides some heft for our ethical principles. No, he insists, God is alive. God is active. And God the Holy Spirit will testify to the truth of the gospel with demonstrations of His power. As you make your way through this book, then, I pray that God will set your heart on fire with the most powerful message ever proclaimed—the message about Jesus Christ and Him crucified.

David F. Watson,
Academic Dean and Professor of New Testament
United Theological Seminary, Dayton, Ohio

INTRODUCTION

The life and death of Jesus of Nazareth has had a greater impact on world history than that of any other person to walk the face of the earth. He is the most controversial person in all of human history. Today, Jesus has more than 2.3 billion people who identify as Christians and follow Him. That is 31 percent of the world's 7.3 billion people.[1] I, too, am a follower of Jesus. I write as a believer, as one who has been transformed by His grace and power, healed by prayer in His name, and blessed to see scores of thousands become followers of Jesus when they or their family or friends were either healed of physical conditions or delivered from demonic bondages.

However, I write not just from my own experience, but as someone who has spent many hours researching and reading thousands of pages about Jesus and the benefits to humanity that are related to His life. He is the primary focus of this book. John Wimber, who was heavily into drugs, alcohol, and rock and roll before becoming a follower of Jesus, used to say to his pastors and leaders in the Vineyard Association of Churches, "Keep the main and plain things the main and plain things of your teaching and ministries." John became the leader of a movement of hundreds of churches, and I was part of that movement for sixteen years. There could be nothing more "main and plain" as the emphasis of Christianity than Jesus.

Having written many books on many subjects, at sixty-eight years of age, my heart is drawn to write a book about Jesus, the founder of Christianity, with a focus on some of the reasons He had to die as He did, on the cross. Together we will explore biblical answers to such questions as: Who was Jesus? Where did He come from? Why did He come? And, more importantly, why did Jesus die, and how do we benefit from His life and death?

When the academic dean of United Theological Seminary heard I was writing on the reasons Jesus had to die, his response was, "That's a difficult subject," and how right he was! There are many interpretations of the life and death of Jesus that tend to be complementary rather than contradictory. Each view can be seen as a different lens through which we study Him. The Orthodox Church, with more than 260 million adherents, approaches the Christian faith with much less rationalism and a greater willingness to accept the mysteries that are beyond our human understanding than do the Roman Catholics and Protestants who make up Western Christianity.

What I write does not succeed in plumbing the fullness of the depths of the many aspects of the life and teachings of Jesus any more than anyone else has done. The magnitude of His death, resurrection, ascension, and continued ministry on our behalf in His glorified state lies somewhere beyond our human understanding. Perhaps, by the grace of God, what I write will in some measure help clear a bit of the fog, allowing us to see Him with greater clarity. Yet, even as we recognize the limitations of human reason in understanding the meaning of Jesus' life, it is important in the twenty-first century to try to focus the images one gets when studying Him, given that most non-Christians have little real understanding of Jesus and the significance of His life, alongside many Christians whose understanding is quite limited. Only as these images are overlaid rather than laid aside and separated from each other are we able to more accurately see the fullness of the meaning of His life.

The four gospels—Matthew, Mark, Luke, and John—are the most important documents we have of Jesus' life, written either by eyewitnesses to His time on this earth or upon a close investigation of those who were eyewitnesses. For this reason I have made them my primary source along with the interpretation of His life given in the remainder of the New Testament. Additionally, I have examined prophecies in the Old Testament as they relate to Jesus and His significance for humanity.

I have purposely avoided the false gnostic gospels rejected by the early church, as their witness to Jesus does not match the truths of the apostolic tradition given by the apostles regarding His teachings and actions. Far from bringing clarity to what we know about Jesus, they mar His image, blur His actions, and dull His words. Thankfully, we have more than two thousand years of reflection by key leaders in the church to draw upon, including seven ecumenical councils made up of the entire church that met to reflect upon correctly understanding Jesus. Most were held to deal with heretical views of Jesus.

Much of the modern understanding of Jesus, while not deemed heretical, has departed from the biblical presentation of Jesus because of philosophical presuppositions that rule out the supernatural. For example, the Jesus Seminar's portrayal of Christ would not have been recognized by the early church. However, in light of all the evidence for the supernatural continuing in church history, it seems there are still many in this world whom Jesus referred to as "while seeing they do not see" (Matt. 13:13 NASB). Jesus is worthy of all praise. He is worthy of our efforts to understand who He was and is, and what He makes available to us through the cross.

I remember being part of the youth group in my Baptist church as we sang the song "There's Something About That Name." Forty-nine years later I am still struck by the power of His name and the power of this song about His name, because the words are so true.

It is my great desire to write the truth about why the name of Jesus is so powerful, why there is "something about that name." So many questions beg to be answered. As we journey together into the heart of Jesus, "let us gaze at Yeshua, him who is The Author and The Perfecter of our faith, who for the joy that was his, endured the cross and ignored the shame, and he sits upon the right side of the throne of God" (Heb. 12:2 ARA).

WHAT DO WE DO WITH SUCH A TRUTH?

The basis for this book began with my daughter's favorite sermon of mine, entitled "Seven Reasons Jesus Had to Die." To date, however, I have never been able to preach past the fourth reason. There is just too much to say about the life, death, and resurrection of Jesus. As I have revisited this topic over the years, it has expanded and is now called "Sixteen Reasons Jesus Had to Die." Even this list of sixteen reasons is not exhaustive. John Piper has a book in which he lists fifty reasons Jesus came to die.

Yet, there is so much more to Jesus than why He was crucified. While the crucifixion is central to our Christian faith, given all the supernatural aspects of Jesus' life and the impact of this life laid down and then raised up again, one has to think that none of it was accidental. Albert Schweitzer was wrong in his view that Jesus was an apocalyptic preacher with a view of the kingdom of God that was more here and now than spiritual. To Schweitzer's way of thinking, the teachings of Jesus simply got out of hand, *accidentally* resulting in His crucifixion. That is a very different picture from the one we find in Scripture. There is nothing accidental about the incarnation, life, death, and resurrection of Jesus.

I want to begin our study with a passage from the gospel of Matthew, chapter 27. Jesus was on trial before the governor, Pontius Pilate. Pilate asked two questions of the crowd who were present at the trial. I believe the sixteen reasons for the death of Jesus outlined in this book answer those questions with a resounding "amen" from heaven! Keep in mind that the crowd was likely composed almost entirely of Jews, except for the Roman guards. Biblical scholars don't know the exact size of the crowd, but estimates place it at two hundred people at most, likely fewer due to how suddenly the trial took place.

Now it was the governor's custom at the festival to release a prisoner chosen by the crowd. At that time they had a well-known prisoner whose name was Jesus Barabbas. [Today we would label Barabbas as a terrorist. Barabbas was an insurrectionist, against the government. He was a murderer and thief, politically motivated.]

So when the crowd had gathered, Pilate asked them, *"Which one do you want me to release to you: Jesus Barabbas, or Jesus who is called the Messiah?"* . . . "Barabbas," they answered. "What shall I do, then, with Jesus who is called the Messiah?" Pilate asked. They all answered, "Crucify him!" *"Why? What crime has he committed?"* asked Pilate. But they shouted all the louder, "Crucify him!"

When Pilate saw that he was getting nowhere, but that instead an uproar was starting, he took water and washed his hands in front of the crowd. "I am innocent of this man's blood," he said. "It is your responsibility!" All the people answered, "His blood is on us and on our children!" Then he released Barabbas to them. But he had Jesus flogged, and handed him over to be crucified. (Matt. 27:15–17, 21–26, emphasis mine)

We have before us two questions to be answered by the life, death, and resurrection of Jesus as found in Scripture.

"Which one do you want me to release to you: Jesus Barabbas, or Jesus who is called the Messiah?"

"Why? What crime has he committed?"

Together, let's look at how Jesus answered those questions.

THE DIVINE INVITATION

Growing up Baptist, I heard evangelistic messages almost every Sunday. Yet, when I heard Matthew 27 preached, the Holy Spirit would convict me of my sin and draw me to give my life to Jesus. I remember the very first time I came under the conviction of the Spirit while listening to this passage. I was quite young at the time, yet even so, God's conviction pierced my heart, causing me to cry. Even though I didn't fully understand it, I was struck by the realization that I was spiritually lost. Being a visually oriented child, I could picture the story in my mind's eye, and it would upset me to the point of tears. How could the people in that crowd ask for Barabbas and reject Jesus? It baffled and upset me.

I remember one night in particular when I was about seven years old. As I sat listening to this passage, I started to cry so much that I rolled over with my face toward the back of the pew so people would think I was sleeping. I didn't want anyone to see me crying. In my mind's eye, I saw the crowd rejecting Jesus, and I heard a new voice—my voice—saying, "Crucify Him!" I knew I was rejecting His call to me. I was doing the same thing the people in the crowd were doing. Here I was, just a young boy with what many might call a short list of sins, but I felt convicted because I was saying no to a divine invitation to surrender my life to the lordship of Jesus Christ.

In my immature mind, I didn't want to cry in public, and I didn't know how I would explain my salvation experience to my younger brother and sister. Those were my silly reasons for resisting God's divine invitation.

Apart from the Holy Spirit knocking at a person's heart, one cannot become a Christian. It's not something you can do by your own will (John 1:12–13). God doesn't have grandchildren, just children. Faith leading to salvation initiates in the divine grace of God where the Spirit comes to you like He came to me when I was seven years old.

I resisted God's call for nine years, until I was one week away from my sixteenth birthday. That was the day grace prevailed, the day my will surrendered to God's call and I gave my life to the Lord. This event marked the beginning of a new trajectory for my life. More on that later.

THE TRIAL OF JESUS AS SEEN IN THE GOSPELS

Returning to our text in the gospel of Matthew, in verse 23, Pilate asked, "Why [should Jesus be crucified]? What crime has he committed?" When you read John's gospel (18:28ff.), you see Pilate trying to avoid crucifying Jesus. He knew Jesus was innocent, having committed no crime worthy of death, so Pilate pleaded to have Jesus beaten instead of crucified, but to no avail. When he saw how desperately the frenzied crowd wanted to crucify Jesus, and fearing a riot if he did not comply, Pilate gave in to their demand rather than risk losing his job. Riots were not allowed by Rome. The crowd that day had been whipped into a frenzy against Jesus by the Jewish leaders who feared Jesus because He had repudiated their legalism and some of their theology. They found Jesus a great threat to their power and authority, and so they turned the people against Him.

Let's reflect for a moment on the first question Pilate asked the crowd:

"Which one do you want me to release to you: Barabbas, or Jesus who is called the Messiah?" On one hand, you have a terrorist who kills, maims, and steals, much like his father the devil. On the other hand, you have Jesus—who heals; encourages; pleads the case of the poor, the marginalized, and women; delivers people from demonization; offers eternal life; and promises His followers the power of the presence of the Holy Spirit as well as the authority to use His name in prayer to the Father. It can be easy to say that *you* would never have chosen Barabbas over Jesus. Yet, truth be told, don't people today still make the wrong choice between Jesus and the prince of this world, the devil? Aren't people still choosing to live in darkness rather than the light, choosing damnation, death, and destruction rather than life eternal, with immortality as a gift?

The answer is yes, people continue to choose Barabbas over Jesus. It should be realized, however, that this decision is not in fact a matter of a mere choice that one can make anytime one desires. It is rather a response to an invitation to open the door to the One who knocks. It doesn't do any good to decide to open the door when no one is knocking. There are two parts to salvation. God does the knocking, and we choose to answer or not. The decision that takes us into life and light is the decision to open *when God is knocking, when He is drawing us.* Make no mistake, God's knock is the most consequential and important opportunity of one's life. It is a divine invitation from a loving Father God.

Pilate's question, "Which one do you want me to release to you: Jesus Barabbas, or Jesus who is called the Messiah?" is a simple question. Yet, I believe we today are more culpable for our answer to that question than the people in the crowd at Jesus' trial. Why? Because the light that you and I have is so much more, so much greater than the light that was available to the crowd who rejected Jesus. The culpability that we have now for our decision is so much greater than theirs. Yes, they had heard and even seen with their own eyes some healings, and so have we. We've seen healings done in Jesus' name and heard thousands of stories and testimonies of miracles and healings done in His name during our lives.

Some in that crowd at the trial may have seen some of Jesus' miracles and healings, but some probably had not. They may have heard Him say that God was His Father, that He was *the Way*, that the only way to the Father was through Him (Jesus). They may have heard that, but so have we. What we have that is so much greater, that makes us more responsible—gives us a greater choice—is the resurrection. The crowd at the trial of Jesus had not yet seen the resurrection of Christ. They knew nothing about His ascension. There was no Pentecost or church of a billion people. We have all these warrants to believe that the crowd at the trial of Jesus did not have. You and I have much greater light than they did.

A question we can ask is, "Why would anyone choose the father of lies?" I believe that the answer is because our hearts and minds become ensnared by the power of sin and the demonic—by the deception of the father of lies, the devil. It is only when we say yes to God's divine invitation that we experience sanctification and begin the process of conforming our minds to the mind of Christ in the power of His Spirit. We will look more closely at sanctification as being both instantaneous and progressive in a later chapter. For now, let's take a brief look at the false claims made against Jesus that led to the cross.

FALSE CLAIMS MADE THAT LED TO JESUS' CRUCIFIXION

In Luke 23, when Pilate asked the crowd what crimes Jesus had committed that would merit death by crucifixion, it is likely that the Sanhedrin, the supreme council and court of the Jews, provided the answers. Let's look at what is said in this regard in Scripture: "And they began to accuse him, saying, 'We have found this man subverting our nation. He opposes payment of taxes to Caesar and claims to be Messiah, a king'" (v. 2).

False: Jesus Perverted the Jewish Nation

In this one verse we find three charges made against Jesus. First is the false charge by the Jewish religious authorities that Jesus perverted the Jewish nation. The underlying reasoning for this stemmed from the Jewish belief that their Messiah would be a conquering king, not a suffering servant. They were looking for a political leader who would conquer their enemies, thereby reestablishing the Jewish nation with peace and prosperity. Jesus' offer of a spiritual victory and God's spiritual kingdom flew in the face of their expectations for their Messiah, so they considered His actions to be perverse.

False: Jesus Opposed Paying Taxes to the Emperor

The second false charge made against Jesus was that He was forbidding them to pay taxes to the emperor. However, in the gospel of Matthew we find Jesus directly addressing this very subject.

> Then the Pharisees went and plotted together how they might trap Him in what He said. And they sent their disciples to Him, along with the Herodians, saying, "Teacher, we know that You are truthful and teach the way of God in truth, and defer to no one; for You are not partial to any. Tell us then, what do You think? Is it lawful to give a poll-tax to Caesar, or not?" . . . And they brought Him a denarius. And He said to them, "Whose likeness and inscription is this?" They said to him, "Caesar's." Then He said to them, "Then render to Caesar the things that are Caesar's; and to God the things that are God's." And hearing this, they were amazed, and leaving Him, they went away. (Matt. 22:15–22 NASB)

Although the Jewish authorities knew their charge that Jesus was forbidding Jews to pay taxes to the emperor was false, nonetheless, by portraying Him as a seditious person, the Jews were betting that the Roman authorities would appear remiss should they not convict Him of sedition.

False: Jesus Committed Treason Against Rome

The third false charge made against Jesus in Luke 23:2 was that He designated Himself to be the Messiah, a king. In John 19:12, when Pilate sought to release Jesus, the Jews objected. "If you release this Man, you are no friend of Caesar; everyone who makes himself out to be a king opposes Caesar" (NASB). Such a claim was considered treason in Rome. The Jews had not succeeded in their attempts to get Pilate to condemn Jesus on political grounds, nor on the charge of blasphemy according to Jewish law. Therefore, they played a trump card by suggesting that Jesus was guilty of treason against Rome. Pilate could not risk such an accusation, and so he acquiesced.

There are a number of other reasons why the Jews opposed Jesus. For instance, there was Jesus' claim that He would destroy the temple and rebuild it again in three days.

> Jesus answered them, "Destroy this temple, and in three days I will raise it up." The Jews then said, "It took forty-six years to build this temple, and will You raise it up in three days?" But He was speaking of the temple of His body. So when He was raised from the dead, His disciples remembered that He said this; and they believed the Scripture and the word which Jesus had spoken. (John 2:19–22 NASB)

This passage is important in our understanding of how Scripture was fulfilled in regard to Jesus' resurrection. While the Jews thought Jesus was speaking of the earthly temple, which was the center of Jewish life and a very holy place, we understand Him to be speaking of His earthly body, which the Jews would destroy, and the resurrection of His glorified body on the third day. Jesus was speaking prophetically, with full understanding and command of the events that were happening and the events that were soon to happen.

Another reason for the Jews' opposition to Jesus was that He spoke forgiveness to people. "Seeing their faith, He said, 'Friend, your sins are forgiven you.' The scribes and the Pharisees began to reason, saying, 'Who is this man who speaks blasphemies? Who can forgive sins, but God alone?'" (Luke 5:20–21 NASB). To speak forgiveness to someone was thought to be something only God could do. Jesus' actions in this regard were considered blasphemy. In speaking forgiveness of sins, Jesus was identifying with the authority and power that belongs to God.

Along with these words and actions, Jesus said and did many other things that became part of His claims of deity, such as His statement "Whoever has seen me has seen the Father" (John 14:9 ESV). This type of blasphemy was punishable by death. If His claims were true, however, He wasn't a blasphemer but rather the divine-human Savior who was and is worthy of our worship, worthy of our surrender.

WHO KILLED JESUS?

False claims against Jesus and the crucifixion are not limited to the trial of Jesus. Historically, there has been a tendency by some to misuse what Scripture is saying in Matthew 27:24–25 regarding who killed Jesus. I think it is important that we in the church have clarity on this point. I am speaking of the rise of anti-Semitism both within and outside the church that came about based on the verses that spoke of the blood of Jesus being on us and our children.

As a church, there is a horrible history of anti-Semitism and our complicity in it. By twisting Scripture, some Christians came to label Jewish people as *Christ killers*. A lot of what Martin Luther wrote about the Jews was later used in Hitler's day to validate the Holocaust in spite of the fact that the early church was entirely Jewish until the Gentiles began coming in. As believers, we must guard our hearts against anti-Semitism and any other use of Scripture to attempt to justify that which is not of God.

Let's be clear about who killed Jesus. *All of us, every single person ever born, is complicit in the death of Jesus.* He died for us, in our place, to do many things for us. It is our sin that is responsible for His death, because Jesus came to do away with sin, to do away with the power of sin, and to destroy the works of the devil. The truth of Scripture is our firm foundation. As the old hymn tells us, Christ is the solid rock on which we stand; all other ground is sinking sand. Each one of us must ultimately make the decision whether or not to stand with Jesus. There is no middle ground to hang out on for all eternity.

NEVER THE GOOD MAN IN THE MIDDLE

It isn't possible to say that Jesus was a good man and at the same time reject His claims of who He is. His claims are so great as to make Him either the biggest liar ever to live or the One to be worshiped. He is either a blasphemer or the Son of God, but never the good man in the middle. We can extend a measure of grace to those in the crowd at His trial because the full revelation of His deity had not been seen on the earth. His resurrection, His ascension, the outpouring of the Spirit at Pentecost, and His appearing to hundreds of people for forty days after His resurrection had not yet occurred.

Therefore, the perspective of the crowd at His trial was somewhat limited. Our perspective of Jesus is much broader. We know the rest of the story. The question is, what do we do with such a truth? What do we do with this Jesus who so graciously comes to knock on the door of our sinful hearts by Word and Spirit? I believe that once a person truly understands all that Jesus accomplished on the cross for them, their only answer will be a resounding, "Yes! Come in!"

Before we begin our examination of the benefits of the cross, I want to look briefly at the identity of Jesus—at who He is. It is important that we understand who hung on the cross if we are to grasp what happened there.

WHO WAS JESUS?

The question "Who was Jesus?" has resonated throughout human history. Before His earthly birth two thousand years ago, the long-awaited Messiah populated the hearts and minds of Old Testament writers to an amazing extent. After His death and resurrection, Jesus was the sole focus of the entire New Testament. It is hard to get away from Jesus even when you try. Mention the name of Jesus and be ready for a fierce conversation. Atheists spend an inordinate amount of time trying to prove that someone they believe never existed doesn't in fact exist. Wise men seek Him, foolish men try to run from Him, and just about everyone who has ever heard His name has an opinion of who He is. The Christian understanding of Jesus is found in the Bible. Other religions, however, have their own "bibles," giving them a different view of Jesus.

The Buddhists don't believe in a personal God, so they obviously do not believe in Jesus as an incarnation of God, or as having divinity. Hindus do not believe Jesus was *the* God. Muslims believe He was a prophet but not the only begotten Son of God in whom the eternal Son incarnated.

New Age religion usually thinks of Jesus as one of many avatars in the company of Krishna, Moses, Gautama Buddha, Confucius, Mohammad, Francis of Assisi, Martin Luther, the Dalai Lama, Helena Blavatsky, Mahatma Gandhi, Sadhu Sundar Sing, Martin Luther King Jr., and Mother Teresa. This view is that the spirit of an avatar is touched and enlightened by the One of the universe, and enlightenment comes upon different people in different generations.

The New Age view of divinity is not personal but pantheistic—the unifying power of the universe that is in all things; more of a Star Wars "may the Force be with you" type of divinity. Atheists don't believe in the divinity of Jesus nor any divinity.

The Star Wars version isn't a biblical understanding of God, because in the Star Wars version the "Force" has both a good side and a bad side. Such a force is similar to Hinduism and New Age religious views that reject Jesus as the divine Savior who was raised from the dead in a glorified body, and as the one who is coming again as the King of kings and Lord of lords to inaugurate His rule and reign over a purified and glorified earth to which heaven has come. All these beliefs about Jesus that are central to Christians are rejected by other religions.

If we reflect again for a moment on the gnostic gospels, written 110 to 300 years after the life of Jesus, we see that they, too, rejected or twisted the claims of Jesus to mean something different from the true biblical understanding of Him as established by the Council of Nicea in AD 325, which recognized the gospels of Matthew, Mark, Luke, and John as the only truly authentic gospels about the actions, teachings, death, and resurrection of Jesus. The fact that these rejected gnostic gospels are in some quarters today being revived and believed is a sign of our times and the impact of postmodern thought.

Though the name of Jesus is honored by His followers who believe there is authority in His name in prayer, nonbelievers use His name to curse. In places where there have been great miracles performed in and through the name of Jesus, His name is held in high honor, as it was in Ephesus (modern-day Turkey), when extraordinary miracles were being done along with great healings and deliverances. As a result of this occasion, "the name of the Lord Jesus was being magnified" (Acts 19:17 NASB). In the New International Version of the Bible, the Greek is translated, "and the name of the Lord Jesus was held in high honor." As we will see, however, not even the performance of miracles causes all to believe in Jesus and His claims about who He was, where He came from, and what He came to do.

In Matthew 11:23, we find strong condemnation from Jesus related to those who had the opportunity to have witnessed His miraculous deeds and continued in their unbelief. "And you people of Capernaum, will you be honored in heaven? No, you will go down to the place of the dead. For if the miracles I did for you had been done in wicked Sodom, it would still be here today" (NLT).

Jesus' statement about the inhabitants of Capernaum and those of Sodom and Gomorrah is shocking. He said it would be better for the people of Sodom and Gomorrah than for those of Capernaum. Why? Because those who lived in Capernaum had the opportunity to see the many miracles and healings Jesus did, and to hear His teaching. Therefore, they had no excuse on the day of judgment.

WHAT DO THE GOSPELS SAY ABOUT JESUS?

"The woman said, 'I know that Messiah' (called Christ) 'is coming. When He comes, He will explain everything to us.' Jesus answered, 'I who speak to you am He'" (John 4:25–26 BSB).

In trying to answer the question of who Jesus was, the best place to begin is in the four gospels of the New Testament. The gospels of Matthew,

Mark, and Luke are referred to as the Synoptic Gospels because of the similarity of their content. The gospel of John stands in contrast with its comparatively distinct content. The Greek term *synoptic* is derived from the Latin *synopsis*, which means "seeing all together." New Testament professor Craig Keener wrote,

> Jesus' mission was completely different from any of the political views about messiahs circulating at the time; "messiahship" was thus an inadequate category for him until he could define it by the character of his mission. His mission could be understood only retrospectively, in the light of his death and resurrection.[2]

It is interesting to note that among the crowds of people who saw and heard Jesus, there were three responses to Him. There were those who rejected His teachings and claims, attributing His supernatural deeds to a demonic source. Then there were those who didn't think He was evil or demonic, but neither did they recognize Him as the Messiah, the Savior, as the Son of Man, the Messianic Prophet who was to come, or as divine. Instead, they merely saw Him as a man, or a good man, a teacher, a carpenter, the son of Joseph and Mary with brothers and sisters. Then there were those who acknowledged Jesus as more than a man, more than a good teacher, more than a prophet, and more than a healer; who saw in Him the fulfillment of Israel's hope—the Messiah, the Son of Man—even God.

The four gospels quite nicely present us with these three perspectives—the negative, neutral, and positive perspectives. In the remaining pages of this introduction, we will briefly examine each.

Although the gospels of Matthew, Mark, and Luke are similar in sequence and oftentimes in wording, each has a different emphasis and a particular audience. Matthew was a disciple of Jesus who wrote primarily to a Jewish audience with an emphasis on Jesus as the next and greater

Moses, and a desire to strengthen Christian Jews who were experiencing suffering. Mark, a scribe of the apostle Peter, wrote to a non-Jewish Roman Christian audience with an emphasis on the power of Jesus, which would have appealed to the Roman emphasis on accomplishment versus the Jewish emphasis on lineage. Luke, a disciple of the apostle Paul, wrote a promotion of Christianity to the Greco-Roman world, and when taken together with the book of Acts, it presents a historical perspective of Jesus with an emphasis on the Passion. John, the beloved disciple, aimed his gospel at Jews and Gentiles who lived throughout the Greco-Roman world with an emphasis on the divinity of Christ.

All three perspectives of Jesus presented to us in the Gospels—negative, neutral, and positive—when taken together, form a lens that affords us a more complete view of Jesus than if we were to ignore any one of the three. Yet, to truly know Jesus to the extent that we are able means to discard every human lens and see Him instead with new eyes in the power of the Spirit. We trust that the gospel writers did just that.

Negative Perspectives of Jesus from Scripture

Jesus was accused:

- Of being a blasphemer and a man who makes Himself out to be God. (Matt. 9:3; 26:65; Mark 2:7; Luke 5:21; John 10:33)
- Of being a glutton and a drunkard. (Matt. 11:19; Luke 7:34)
- Of being a friend of tax collectors and sinners. (Matt. 9:10–11; 11:19; Mark 2:15–16; Luke 5:30; 7:34)
- Of having lost His senses. (Mark 3:21)
- Of being possessed by Beelzebub (the prince of demons). (Matt. 12:24, 27; Mark 3:22; Luke 11:15, 18–19)

- Of leading multitudes away from the true faith or from God; of being an evildoer. (John 18:30)
- Of being a Samaritan and having a demon. (Matt. 9:34)
- Of not only having a demon but also being insane. (John 10:20)
- Of being a man who was not from God because He did not keep the Sabbath. (Matt. 12:1–2; Mark 1:21; 2:23–24)
- Of perverting the nation and being a sinner. (Matt. 17:17; Luke 9:41)

Let's break down each of these accusations a bit in order to better understand some of what was behind them. First, Jesus was accused of being a blasphemer because He said things about Himself that were attributes of God. To summarize, He said He had come from God, and that He existed before His birth. He used language that identified Himself as the God of the Jews, the *I Am*. He claimed God was His Father, and that His words and actions were done under the direction of God, His Father. His actions to forgive sin were a divine prerogative. Therefore, if He was not divine, He was a blasphemer.

The accusation that Jesus was a glutton and a drunkard was based on the fact that He didn't fast as the Pharisees did, and because He went to the homes of sinners and fellowshiped with them, and even ate and drank with them. These actions tied into the accusations that He was a friend of sinners.

The charge of having lost His senses or being insane or raving mad were due to Jesus' statements about Himself that pertained to His being the "gate for the sheep," and the "shepherd [who] lays down his life for the sheep." In context, in John 9–10, especially 10:6–21, Jesus had just restored sight to a man born blind. This act of healing was followed by His claims that the Father loved Him because He was willing to lay down

His life for the sheep, and then to exercise the authority to take up His life again. This was a reference to His death and resurrection.

Jesus was accused of being demon possessed or of being the "prince of the demons" because He performed healings, miracles, and deliverances that were beyond human ability. In other words, the accusation was that His power must be demonic rather than divine, unless of course He was actually the divine Son of God.

Accusations that He was leading the nation (the Jews) astray or away from God were based upon His teachings and actions that challenged and accused the religious authorities of being blind guides and hired hands that run away from the flock, rather than true shepherds. In truth, Jesus was a threat to the views of the Sadducees and the Pharisees, and the scribes and teachers of the law. Judaism, at that time, was a cessationist belief system that maintained that although God had at one time spoken to His people through prophets and performed miracles, prophecies and miracles had ceased. Only the Old Testament scriptures remained to guide God's people. Both Jesus' teachings and His miracles were a threat to the Jewish religious system of the day.

These negative statements—these *ad hominem* (against the man) arguments—were meant to discredit the testimony of Jesus and those who gave witness to who He was. Today we would call them "fake news" meant as character assassination to discredit Jesus.

While Jesus' actions were confusing and threatening to those without eyes to see or ears to hear, Jesus Himself was quite clear about what He was doing. He was redirecting the people of God away from the status quo, away from the old covenant, and preparing them for the new covenant that would be enacted by Him with the shedding of His blood. He was doing all that was necessary to bring about the new covenant Spirit with whom He would baptize His followers, and which would result in a radical shift in the people of God. There was coming a new reality in His kingdom as a result of Pentecost that would follow the first Easter morning. With this in mind, let's take a look at the neutral perspectives of Jesus as found in the New Testament.

Neutral Perspectives of Jesus from Scripture

The people who saw and heard Jesus during His earthly ministry often responded with a neutral perspective, unsure of who He was or what He was about. Unlike their negative counterparts, they didn't see Him as evil, but neither were they willing to embrace Him as divine. Instead, they referred to Him in a variety of ways.

- Jesus the Nazarene or a Nazarene (Matt. 2:23b; Mark 10:47; 14:67b; 16:16; Luke 24:19; John 18:5a, 7; 19:19; Acts 2:22; 3:6; 4:10; 6:14; 22:8)
- Rabboni, teacher, rabbi, and a good teacher (Matt. 12:38; 19:16; 22:16, 36)
- The carpenter or carpenter's son, the son of Mary, and the brother of James, Joseph, Simon, and Judas (Matt. 13:55; Mark 6:3)
- Jesus of Nazareth and the son of Joseph (Matt. 21:11; 26:71; Mark 1:9, 24; Luke 4:22, 34; 18:37; John 1:45; 6:24; Acts 10:38; 26:9)
- King of the Jews (Matt. 2:2, 11; 27:29; Mark 15:2; Luke 23:3)
- A good teacher and a good man (Mark 10:17; John 7:12)

While these neutral perspectives of Jesus did not necessarily denigrate Him, like their negative counterparts, those who held a neutral perspective of Jesus lacked the eyes to see and ears to hear what God was saying and doing in their midst. In the book of Revelation, John made clear how our Lord views the person who is neither hot nor cold—rejection by God is their fate: "So because you are lukewarm, and neither hot nor cold, I will spit you out of My mouth" (Rev. 3:16 NASB).

Positive Perspectives of Jesus from Scripture

Positive perspectives of Jesus abound in the Gospels. The gospel writers have given us an amazing glimpse of the Jesus they either knew personally from their time with Him during His earthly ministry and in His resurrected body, or from accounts of people who knew Him personally. What emerges is a picture of a glorious Lord and Savior. As you take in these scriptures[3] (including a few from the Old Testament), may your heart soar with praise and thanksgiving to the One who set us free and lives so that we, too, might live.

- **Advocate**——"My dear children, I write this to you so that you will not sin. But if anybody does sin, we have an advocate with the Father——Jesus Christ, the Righteous One." (1 John 2:1)
- **Almighty One**——" . . . who is, and who was, and who is to come, the Almighty." (Rev. 1:8)
- **Alpha and Omega**——"I am the Alpha and the Omega, the First and the Last, the Beginning and the End." (Rev. 22:13)
- **Author and Perfecter of Our Faith**——"Fixing our eyes on Jesus, the author and perfecter of faith, who for the joy set before Him endured the cross, despising the shame, and has sat down at the right hand of the throne of God." (Heb. 12:2 NASB)
- **Authority**——"Then Jesus came to them and said, 'All authority in heaven and on earth has been given to me.'" (Matt. 28:18)
- **Beloved Son of God**——"And behold, a voice out of the heavens said, 'This is My beloved Son, in whom I am well-pleased.'" (Matt. 3:17 NASB)
- **Bread of Life**——"Then Jesus declared, 'I am the bread of life. Whoever comes to me will never go hungry, and whoever believes in me will never be thirsty.'" (John 6:35)
- **Bridegroom**——"And Jesus said to them, 'Can the wedding guests

mourn as long as the bridegroom is with them? The days will come when the bridegroom is taken away from them, and then they will fast.'" (Matt. 9:15 ESV)

- **Chief Cornerstone**—"The stone which the builders rejected has become the chief corner stone." (Ps. 118:22 NASB)
- **Deliverer**—"And to wait for his Son from heaven, whom he raised from the dead, Jesus who delivers us from the wrath to come." (1 Thess. 1:10 ESV)
- **Faithful and True**—"I saw heaven standing open and there before me was a white horse, whose rider is called Faithful and True. With justice he judges and wages war." (Rev. 19:11)
- **Good Shepherd**—"I am the good shepherd. The good shepherd lays down his life for the sheep." (John 10:11)
- **Great High Priest**—"Therefore, since we have a great high priest who has passed through the heavens, Jesus the Son of God, let us hold fast our confession." (Heb. 4:14 NASB)
- **Head of the Church**—"And he put all things under his feet and gave him as head over all things to the church." (Eph. 1:22 ESV)
- **Holy Servant**—" . . . and grant that Your bond-servants may speak Your word with all confidence, while You extend Your hand to heal, and signs and wonders take place through the name of Your holy servant Jesus." (Acts 4:29–30 NASB)
- **I Am**—"Jesus said to them, 'Truly, truly, I say to you, before Abraham was born, I am.'" (John 8:58 NASB)
- **Immanuel**—" . . . She will give birth to a son and will call him Immanuel (which means 'God is with us')." (Isa. 7:14 NLT)
- **Indescribable Gift**—"Thanks be to God for His indescribable gift!" (2 Cor. 9:15 NASB)
- **Judge**—" . . . he is the one whom God appointed as judge of the living and the dead." (Acts 10:42)

- **King of Kings**—"These will wage war against the Lamb, and the Lamb will overcome them, because He is Lord of lords and King of kings, and those who are with Him are the called and chosen and faithful." (Rev. 17:14 NASB)
- **Lamb of God**—"The next day John saw Jesus coming toward him and said, 'Look, the Lamb of God, who takes away the sin of the world!'" (John 1:29)
- **Light of the World**—"I am the light of the world. Whoever follows me will never walk in darkness, but will have the light of life." (John 8:12)
- **Lion of the Tribe of Judah**—"Weep no more; behold, the Lion of the tribe of Judah, the Root of David, has conquered, so that he can open the scroll and its seven seals." (Rev. 5:5 ESV)
- **Lord of All**—"For this reason also, God highly exalted Him, and bestowed on Him the name which is above every name, so that at the name of Jesus every knee will bow, of those who are in heaven and on earth and under the earth, and that every tongue will confess that Jesus Christ is Lord, to the glory of God the Father." (Phil. 2:9–11 NASB)
- **Mediator**—"For there is one God, and one mediator also between God and men, the man Christ Jesus." (1 Tim. 2:5 NASB)
- **Messiah**—"'We have found the Messiah' (that is, the Christ)." (John 1:41)
- **Mighty One**—"Then you will know that I, the LORD, am your Savior, your Redeemer, the Mighty One of Jacob." (Isa. 60:16)
- **One Who Sets Free**—"So if the Son sets you free, you will be free indeed." (John 8:36)
- **Our Hope**—". . . Christ Jesus our hope." (1 Tim. 1:1)
- **Peace**—"For he himself is our peace, who has made the two groups one and has destroyed the barrier, the dividing wall of hostility." (Eph. 2:14)

- **Prophet**—"Jesus said to them, 'A prophet is not without honor except in his hometown and among his own relatives and in his own household.'" (Mark 6:4 NASB)
- **Redeemer**—"As for me, I know that my Redeemer lives, and at the last He will take His stand on the earth." (Job 19:25 NASB)
- **Resurrection and the Life**—"Jesus said to her, 'I am the resurrection and the life. The one who believes in me will live, even though they die.'" (John 11:25)
- **Risen Lord**—" . . . that Christ died for our sins according to the Scriptures, that he was buried, that he was raised on the third day according to the Scriptures." (1 Cor. 15:3–4)
- **Rock**—" . . . for they drank from the spiritual rock that accompanied them, and that rock was Christ." (1 Cor. 10:4)
- **Sacrifice for Our Sins**—"This is love: not that we loved God, but that he loved us and sent his Son as an atoning sacrifice for our sins." (1 John 4:10)
- **Savior**—"For unto you is born this day in the city of David a Saviour, which is Christ the Lord." (Luke 2:11 KJV)
- **Son of Man**—"For the Son of Man came to seek and to save the lost." (Luke 19:10)
- **Son of the Most High**—"He will be great and will be called the Son of the Most High. The Lord God will give him the throne of his father David." (Luke 1:32)
- **Supreme Creator Over All**—"For by Him all things were created, both in the heavens and on earth, visible and invisible, whether thrones or dominions or rulers or authorities—all things have been created through Him and for Him. He is before all things, and in Him all things hold together." (Col. 1:16–17 NASB)
- **The Door**—"I am the door; if anyone enters through Me, he will be saved, and will go in and out and find pasture." (John 10:9 NASB)

- **The Way**—"Jesus answered, 'I am the way and the truth and the life. No one comes to the Father except through me.'" (John 14:6)
- **The Word**—"In the beginning was the Word, and the Word was with God, and the Word was God." (John 1:1)
- **True Vine**—"I am the true vine, and My Father is the vinedresser." (John 15:1 NASB)
- **Truth**—"Then you will know the truth, and the truth will set you free." (John 8:32)
- **Victorious One**—"To the one who is victorious, I will give the right to sit with me on my throne, just as I was victorious and sat down with my Father on his throne." (Rev. 3:21)
- **Wonderful Counselor, Mighty God, Everlasting Father, Prince of Peace**—"For to us a child is born, to us a son is given, and the government will be on his shoulders. And he will be called Wonderful Counselor, Mighty God, Everlasting Father, Prince of Peace." (Isa. 9:6)

Although this is not an exhaustive list of the names and attributes of Jesus from Scripture, I believe it is sufficient for the purposes of this book, in order for us to understand His identity particularly in light of the cross.

Clearly, for those with eyes to see and ears to hear, the Bible gives us a great deal of information about the identity of Jesus while leaving us to wrestle with the reality that "For now we see in a mirror, dimly, but then face to face. Now I know in part, but then I shall know just as I also am known" (1 Cor. 13:12 NKJV). O, how glorious the full vision of Jesus will be!

SIXTEEN REASONS JESUS HAD TO DIE

With a picture fresh in our minds of the false claims made against Jesus by the Jews at His trial, and a brief examination of Jesus' identity from the Gospels, let us turn our attention to what I understand to be sixteen reasons Jesus had to die. As I mentioned earlier, this is not a complete list by any stretch of the imagination. That being said, I do believe that this list provides information that is central to our understanding of what took place on the cross as it pertains to believers. Further, it is my prayer that any nonbelievers who read this book will find these reasons so compelling as to cause them to seek Jesus as their Lord and Savior. Let's examine them, chapter by chapter.

In the first chapter, we will begin our examination with a focus on how Jesus defeats and destroys the works of the devil—specifically, how His death destroyed those things that attempt to keep us in bondage: demons, drugs, and other addictions.

one

JESUS DIED TO DESTROY CAPTIVITY

Demons, Drugs, and Other Addictions

Then Jesus came to Nazareth, where He had been brought up.
As was His custom, He entered the synagogue on the Sabbath.
And when He stood up to read, the scroll of the prophet Isaiah
was handed to Him. Unrolling it, He found the place where it was
written: "The Spirit of the Lord is on Me, because He has anointed
Me to preach good news to the poor. He has sent Me to proclaim
liberty to the captives and recovery of sight to the blind, to release
the oppressed, to proclaim the year of the Lord's favor."
—LUKE 4:16–19 BSB

As we study Jesus' march toward the cross, in Luke 9 (and also in Matthew and Mark) we find Jesus with His face set toward Jerusalem. Passover was almost upon the Jewish people and the *once-and-forever Paschal Lamb* (Jesus) was about to be sacrificed. Many speak of the will of the Father in all of this. If the crucifixion of Jesus was the will of the Father, our question can be, "Why? Why did God will the crucifixion?" One reason God the Father sent His Son Jesus to the cross was to set us free from the captivity of the devil that manifests through demons, drugs, and other addictions.

The death of Jesus was no accident. It was planned within the Trinity before the creation of the universe. Colossians 1:15 tells us, "[Jesus] is the image of the invisible God, the firstborn of all creation" (NASB). A study was done by Ramsay MacMillan, a secular historian from Yale University, who wrote *Christianizing the Roman Empire*.[1] He wanted to find out how Christianity became the official religion of the Roman Empire, especially since there were other gods and Christianity was an illegal religion. How did it become the official religion of the Roman Empire? The number one reason was the power of the gospel to set people free from demons. Number two was the power of the gospel to heal the sick. Those two signs caused people to believe the gospel, then, having believed, they became part of the church. In this chapter we will examine the power of the gospel to set people free from demonic captivity.

THE CROSS DELIVERS US FROM EVIL

The blood of Jesus as the Paschal Lamb, the Lamb of God slain from the foundation of the world, brings deliverance from the captivity of the devil. When Christians celebrate Holy Communion with bread and wine, we "eat" His flesh and "drink" His blood as the Israelites ate the flesh of the Paschal lamb and sprinkled the blood of the lamb on their doorposts as protection from evil and death. This imagery of an innocent lamb's blood applied to our "house" (each individual believer is a dwelling place for Christ) symbolizes the sacrifice of Jesus for all. The act of participating in Communion provides a mystical union with Christ for Christian believers. Within this union is the power of His yielded body, the blood of

Jesus to wash away our sins, and the flesh of Jesus to bring healing and wholeness to us both physically and spiritually—through physical healing and inner healing of emotions.

In Exodus 12:27 we see that it is the sacrifice of the Paschal lamb that spared the faithful as the Lord passed over the houses of the people of Israel in Egypt. Jewish faith celebrates this event with the most significant celebration of their calendar year, the Passover festival, an annual observance of their deliverance from slavery in Egypt under the leadership of Moses. For Christian believers, the true meaning of Passover is found in remembering the sacrifice of Jesus (Yeshua), "the Lamb of God, who takes away the sin of the world" (John 1:29). It is in this sense that Moses was a type of Jesus, a deliverer who led the people of God out of human slavery.

It was no small miracle that the Israelites were delivered from the Egyptian army, the most powerful military force in the world of that day. God used Moses, a former shepherd, to deliver, with many signs and wonders. Yet Moses is but a shadow of the One to come—Jesus.

THE SUPREMACY OF CHRIST

Paul, in his letter to the church in Colossae, urged believers to remember how Jesus defeated and destroyed the works of the devil so that he no longer holds power over one's spirit, soul, and body. "When He had disarmed the rulers and authorities, He made a public display of them, having triumphed over them through Him" (Col. 2:15 NASB). Let's look a little more closely at the supremacy of Christ as found in Colossians 1.

> He is the image of the invisible God, the firstborn of all creation; for in him all things in heaven and on earth were created, things visible and invisible whether thrones or dominions or rulers or powers—all things

have been created through him and for him. He himself is before all things, and in him all things hold together. He is the head of the body, the church; he is the beginning, the firstborn from the dead, so that he might come to have first place in everything. For in him all the fullness of God was pleased to dwell, and through him God was pleased to reconcile to himself all things, whether on earth or in heaven, by making peace through the blood of his cross. (vv. 15–20 NRSV)

The cross of Christ and all its benefits is the hope set before us by God Himself in His glorious plan of redemption. Such an unfathomable gift cries out for an all-consuming response, that we die to sin and live in and for Christ. The power of the finished work—the disarming of the rulers and authorities and the triumph over them on the cross—enables us to do this.

JESUS CAME TO SET THE CAPTIVES FREE

In my years of ministry, time and again I have been privileged to see people set free from the grip of the devil by the power of Jesus. In a previous book I wrote,

God in His great love desires that all His beloved sons and daughters live in freedom, unbound from the schemes of the enemy. Jesus paid for this freedom on the cross. His earthly ministry was a constant demonstration of the authority of God over the devil and his minions. . . . *"For God so loved the world that he gave his one and only Son"* (John 3:16). When the Word became flesh, light came into the world. This light shines in the darkness and will not be extinguished. Jesus, the light of the world, came to bind up the brokenhearted and set the captives free (Luke 4:18). He is still doing this work today through His bride, the church.[2]

I remember the time I was contacted by a man I knew in high school. This guy had been a drug pusher. When revival broke out in the church I grew up in, I found this guy, told him about Jesus, and invited him to the revival. He came and was saved out of his drug addiction, then later was called to preach. We went on to college together, to study for ministry. Sadly, at one point, he dropped out of seminary and fell away from the Lord.

Some forty years had passed when he called me. As we talked, he told me that he was proud of me because of what God had done in and through my life. Then he told me about his struggle with post-traumatic stress disorder (PTSD). He had been drafted during the Vietnam War and served in Cambodia. It was during that time that he saw a friend blown up by a mortar. PTSD had been his constant companion since that day. He had been saved and delivered from addiction, but couldn't escape the horrors of PTSD. It destroyed two marriages and brought terrible nightmares and all the other classic symptoms that come with severe mental trauma.

I was able to connect him with my friend Dr. Mike Hutchings, director of our campus training school, who walks in a strong anointing for healing of PTSD. Mike was able to minister to this man, and he was gloriously set free from the grip of demonic oppression that had manifested as PTSD.

On another occasion, during a ministry trip to Brazil, one of our team members began to minister to a young man who had all but lost vision in his left eye. He could only read by covering his left eye, and even then his vision was limited. As they talked, the man shared that his mother had at one time put a curse on him. Our team member renounced the curse in the name of Jesus and the man's vision was restored. He was able to read clearly, even when he covered his right eye. There is power in the blood of Jesus to set every captive free!

MY OWN INTRODUCTION TO DELIVERANCE

Heidi and Rolland Baker have many powerful testimonies of deliverance from their years in ministry. One such testimony has deeply impacted me. I want to share it here in my own words.

During an outreach in Mozambique, Heidi's team was approached by a man named Jose and his girlfriend, Albertina, who had lost her fingers and toes due to leprosy. At the time of this encounter, both Jose and Albertina were practicing witch doctors. Thanks be to God that this day was to be their day of deliverance. They are now dear friends of Heidi and followers of Jesus.

On that day, Jose approached the outreach team with three venomous snakes with the goal of disrupting their visit. As Heidi spoke to him, the Lord gave her a word for him. "Aren't you tired of darkness?" she asked. "Do you want to come into the light?" When he indicated that he did, Heidi said she had to kill his snakes. As this interaction was happening, a member of her team saw the glory of God on top of Jose.

People dug a hole in the ground, put the snakes in the hole, and burned them to death. As the serpents were burning, venom and blood came out of Jose's hands because he'd been bitten many times. God completely healed him. While all this was going on, God put glory and peace around Jose and Albertina. After that, both of them came to Jesus.

Heidi asked Jose if he wanted to be baptized, and he said yes he did. Then she asked if he and Albertina wanted to be married, and they said, "Yes, before God." The Lord told Heidi to give Albertina a ruby and diamond ring and tell the woman she was a princess. They said their wedding vows down by the water, and they were baptized.

The village had been so afraid of this man, but now he was set free. The entire village had witnessed him come to know Jesus as his Savior, marry his girlfriend who had also been saved, and be baptized with his new wife. Jose said, "I am leaving all of my past life to follow the Lord, and to have a new life in God. I was a very strong witch doctor, and now I come to hear the word of the Lord, to receive the anointing of the Lord, and to have a new life." He went on to say that when he was baptized, he felt a completely different Spirit and he was changed. When he was saved, he learned about love.

The New Testament reveals that Satan is a defeated foe. The apostle Paul tells us that "the God of peace will soon crush Satan under your feet" (Rom. 16:20) so that "neither death nor life, nor angels nor rulers, nor things present nor things to come, nor powers, nor height nor depth, nor anything else in all creation, will be able to separate us from the love of God in Christ Jesus our Lord" (Rom. 8:38–39 ESV).

It is important to remember that were it not for the cross of Christ, each one of us would remain captive to Satan—poor, blind, wretched, and oppressed unto death. All of our triumphs are in Christ! Paul knew this truth, which he so joyously proclaimed in his second letter to the Corinthians as his personal reason for his beliefs and actions—his *apologia pro vita sua* (a defense of his life): "But thanks be to God, who always leads us in triumph in Christ, and manifests through us the sweet aroma of the knowledge of Him in every place" (2 Cor. 2:14 NASB).

In answer to Pilate's question of why Jesus had to die, Scripture says that Jesus died to destroy captivity in the form of demons, drugs, and other addictions.

two

JESUS DIED TO RELEASE THE POWER AND AUTHORITY TO HEAL

And when the men of that place recognized Jesus, they sent word to all the surrounding country. People brought all their sick to him and begged him to let the sick just touch the edge of his cloak, and all who touched it were healed.

—MATTHEW 14:35–36

The Gospels abound with examples of Jesus as the healer. In the fullness of the gospel itself—the life, death, and resurrection of Jesus—we are afforded forgiveness and eternal life as well as supernatural healing, deliverance, and miracles. All of these aspects of the cross are available to believers. Yet, if we don't discern what Jesus has done in His body for us—"By His stripes we are healed" (Isa. 53:5 NKJV)—we will have faith for forgiveness and eternal life, but not faith for healing.

The body of Jesus, given for us on the cross—scourged and crucified—carried our sicknesses and diseases. There is forgiveness in the blood of

Jesus and healing in the body of Jesus. If we discern what He did through His blood shed on the cross but don't discern the value of His body given for us, then we won't appropriate all that is available to us through the cross. The benefits of His death are not an either/or choice, but a both/and. This is important for believers to understand. Yet, much of the church struggles with this truth. Let's look to Scripture for clarity, beginning in the Old Testament where Jesus is foreshadowed again and again.

JEHOVAH WHO HEALS

In Exodus 15:26, God tells us that He is Jehovah Rapha, the "LORD, who heals you." *Jehovah* is a derivative of the Hebrew *Havah*, which means "to exist" or "to be." *Rapha* in Hebrew means "to make healthful," "to heal," "to restore." *Strong's Concordance* denotes *rapha* as a verb that means "to heal," "become fresh," "repaired." The Aramaic translates it as "darn, mend, repair, . . . stitch together."[1] Together, *Jehovah Rapha* translates to "Jehovah Who Heals."

Why is it a stretch for so many to think that Jesus, the only Son of God, the Lamb of God given for us, would effect a continuum of God's healing for those who believe on Him? When God delivered His people from captivity in Egypt, He made His healing available to them. As Moses cast the tree into the bitter waters of Marah according to God's directive, the waters became sweet for the people of God, who pronounced Himself as the One who heals those who keep His statutes.

Likewise, the cross of Christ—the bitterness of the cross—effects the "sweetness" of God toward those who believe on His Son, as it continues to make His healing available to us, as well as His forgiveness. In John 14:7 Jesus said, "If you had known Me, you would have known My Father also; from now on you know Him, and have seen Him" (NASB).

JESUS OUR PASCHAL LAMB

Let's look more closely at what happened to the people of God in the exodus. Psalm 105:37 says, "He brought them forth also with silver and gold: and there was not one feeble person among their tribes" (KJV). Most translations say, "no one stumbled," but older translations say, "there were no feeble ones." One translation says that there were no sick among them. Sick people are typically feeble, and they often stumble. So you have some two million Hebrew people who came out of captivity during the exodus and there was not one sick person among them; not one weak person; not one person who stumbled? That is truly miraculous!

How did this happen? I believe the answer is found in the divine instructions given to the people of God before the exodus. "Then they are to take some of the blood and put it on the sides and tops of the doorframes of the houses where they eat the lambs. That same night they are to eat the meat roasted over the fire, along with bitter herbs, and bread made without yeast" (Ex. 12:7–8). In the latter part of verse 11, the people are instructed to eat in haste as it is the Lord's Passover. The instructions continue in verse 46: "It must be eaten inside the house; take none of the meat outside the house. Do not break any of the bones." The scripture is talking about the Paschal lamb that each Hebrew household was instructed to sacrifice and then eat.

Jesus is our Paschal Lamb, the New Testament typology of Moses who prefigured Christ. The difference is, Jesus succeeded on the cross, triumphing where Israel failed. Jesus is our Paschal meal. The apostle Paul put it thus:

> For I received from the Lord what I also passed on to you: The Lord Jesus, on the night he was betrayed, took bread, and when he had given thanks, he broke it and said, "This is my body, which is for you; do this in remembrance of me." In the same way, after supper he took the cup, saying, "This cup is the new covenant in my blood; do this, whenever you drink

it, in remembrance of me." For whenever you eat this bread and drink this cup, you proclaim the Lord's death until he comes. So then, whoever eats the bread or drinks the cup of the Lord in an unworthy manner will be guilty of sinning against the body and blood of the Lord. Everyone ought to examine themselves before they eat of the bread and drink from the cup. For those who eat and drink without discerning the body of Christ eat and drink judgment on themselves. That is why many among you are weak and sick, and a number of you have fallen asleep. (1 Cor. 11:23–30)

What this says to me is that believers who partake of the bread of Communion—who "eat" the body of Christ—without recognizing the fullness of what He accomplished in His physical body on the cross for our healing, are guilty of not recognizing the unity of the body and blood. The blood of Christ was shed for our forgiveness, and the body was given for our healing. When we don't discern the fullness of the cross, we end up with a truncated faith—with faith for forgiveness but not for healing.

HEALING IS PERSONAL

My personal interest in the healing that is available to us from the cross began with several incidents from my childhood. The first was my grandmother's healing. When I was a small child, she was sovereignly healed of a large goiter by the hand of God. No one prayed for her. She simply acted in obedience to the voice of God when He told her to go into the bedroom and pray. When she obeyed, He healed her. Her simple yet powerful testimony made a distinct impression on me that would later pique my growing interest in healing.

The second healing miracle that impacted me significantly as a child happened to my favorite Sunday school teacher. I was twelve years old when she was diagnosed with a very large cancerous tumor. She was a woman of great faith who had a strong personal relationship with Jesus. The church prayed for her, and the next day, when she went in for surgery, the "very large" tumor had shrunk to the size of an orange. It was easily removed and no more cancer was found in her body.

The third incident involved my grandfather. I was fifteen at the time he was diagnosed with cancer. He was a heavy smoker who smoked two packs of unfiltered cigarettes a day and had a very unhealthy diet. At the time there was very little knowledge about the connection between things like cigarettes, diet, and cancer. We prayed, the church prayed, everyone prayed. Grandpa wanted to live so badly and fought a valiant fight, but he died at sixty-four years of age. After that healing became a great mystery to me. The same people who prayed for my Sunday school teacher prayed for my grandpa, yet he wasn't healed. I didn't understand it.

Then, when I was in my mid-teens, I heard my first sermon on healing preached by, of all things, a Baptist pastor. He had started out somewhere as a Methodist and later joined the General Baptist Church, the denomination in which I was raised. We didn't have sermons in my church on healing. For the first time in my life I was hearing teachings about healing. At the end of the sermon he invited people who needed healing to come forward and then he laid hands on them and prayed for healing. He got in trouble for praying for the sick as a Baptist because they didn't believe there was such a gift. I wondered, "Why is he in trouble if healing the sick is in the Bible?"

BORN AGAIN AND HEALED

So there I was, a sixteen-year-old, struggling to understand healing, and fighting with myself to surrender my will to God (since that first divine invitation when I was seven years old) with no idea that I was about to experience both. My surrender happened just one week shy of my sixteenth birthday. I'll never forget that night. I had white-knuckled the pew from the age of seven to that night, trying not to cry, telling God I wanted "to become a Christian when I was older, but not now." My heart had become hardened, my conscience seared. I could no longer detect the divine invitation from the Holy Spirit calling me to renounce my sin and give my life to Jesus. I had been sitting in the same church, hearing the same gospel, and yet it might as well have been the Gettysburg Address I was hearing. I felt no tears, no sorrow, no conviction, nothing. I was dead to the Holy Spirit, unable to hear the One knocking on my door.

Then I remembered something my dad had shared with me years earlier. There was a man who came to our house who told my dad that he couldn't feel anything and was worried about his soul. My dad told him to seek God, to ask God to convict him again, to give him another chance. With my dad's words in front of me, I started to pray.

"Lord," I said, "I've said no to You so many times. I've hardened my heart. I know Your Word says that Your Spirit won't always strive with people; that we can become so hardened that You give up and leave us alone. My biggest issue is pride. I don't want to cry in public. Every time You have drawn me, I say no because of my pride. God, what I really want is for You to convict me, draw me so strongly and let Your grace be so irresistible that I can't say no. Break my pride and just save me! If I tell You to leave me alone, don't listen!"

God heard the cry of my heart that day, and less than a month later He answered that prayer, but not in the way I expected. He brought me under conviction through my great uncle Reno who had Down syndrome. Because I had grown up out in the country and there weren't many other kids to play with, Uncle Reno had become my play buddy. He had the mentality of a nine-year-old and we had a lot of fun together.

One night in church Uncle Reno stood up and, in spite of a severe stutter, testified saying, "I want R-R-R-Randy R-R-Ray to be s-s-s-saved." Tears filled my eyes as the conviction of God began to overtake my heart. Those of us who were experiencing the conviction of the Holy Spirit were asked to come up front to shake the pastor's hand. We formed a line and walked right in front of the mourner's bench and stood in front of the pulpit. Deacons (spiritual leaders of the church) stood on both sides of the pastor. They knew I was the oldest unsaved person in the church. When it was my turn to stand in front of them, each one asked me, "Randy, don't you want to give your life to Jesus?"

"Yes," I replied, "but not tonight."

Meanwhile, my grandfather had gone over to the "Amen" corner. I decided I'd go sit by him. I was really glad he didn't say anything. Ever since Uncle Reno had spoken, God had been dealing with me, convicting me, and I was struggling. Then my Sunday school teacher, whom we called Sister Imogene, came over. Oftentimes, in a Baptist church, if you feel like God is dealing with someone for salvation, if the Holy Spirit leads you, you go to the person and start talking to them about their soul. Sister Imogene put her arm around my shoulder and said, "Honey, don't you know how much Jesus loves you?" That's when God answered my prayer.

I started weeping out loud and literally ran to the altar, got on my knees, and prayed until I was born again. I prayed until I didn't feel guilty anymore. I prayed until the Holy Spirit came into me and I felt peace and joy and totally new. That's how I knew I had been born again, saved. Yet, there was more to come, much more. I would backslide, rededicate my life, and struggle until the day of my car accident. Many of you have heard of or read about my healing testimony. However, for those who haven't, here it is. I tell it over and over again because it brings God glory.

MY OWN HEALING

Seeing others healed by God is one thing. You can believe it wholeheartedly or wonder if it was in fact God or just a coincidence, or a mixture of the two. You can puzzle at the teachings of the church that don't line up with scripture regarding healing. However, when God heals you, everything changes. Suddenly you know that God heals. You may not fully understand how it all works or the theology behind it, but your healing speaks volumes that cannot be silenced.

I had seen a few healings during my childhood and heard some preaching on healing, but it remained a mystery to me in many respects until I received it myself. It happened as a result of a car accident when I was in college. Two days before the accident I had rededicated my life to God again with Fred, the youth director and song leader for the church I had attended since sixteen. I packed up my drugs and gave them to him and broke up with my girlfriend.

My friends George and Joe, and Joe's sister, were in the car with me when a friend started to pass me, lost control of his car, and slammed into mine, knocking me off the road and into a concrete embankment. Joe was thrown from the car and died. I was seriously injured. I had multiple fractures in my forehead and three places along my hairline were crushed. My jaw was broken along with the bone underneath one eyebrow. I had a compressed vertebrae, neurological damage in my spine, and fractured ribs. My digestive system and my kidneys stopped working.

Doctors put fifty stitches in my face, considered putting a metal plate in my skull, pumped my stomach because my digestive system had shut down, and pumped me full of Demerol every three hours to deal with the pain. When my digestive system didn't restart itself after a few days, doctors made plans to transfer me to another hospital that could more adequately give me care. Meanwhile, my youth group had been praying for me.

The first hint that God was healing me was when the doctor came to set my broken jaw and found it was already set. The next day my digestive system started working. At first, I didn't connect the dots. That is, until I was well enough to start reading the Bible with reflective glasses because that was the only way I could read while lying flat on my back. Because of the swelling in my spine, I was not allowed to put a pillow under my head, sit up, or move. Two days later all my pain was gone. That's when it really hit me—God was healing me! My church youth group had prayed, and after that my healing happened over a period of days. First, my jaw was sovereignly set, then my digestive system was healed, and then I was healed of all pain. That's when I heard God say, "I have healed you. Get out of bed and walk." I was released five days later, after waiting for a brace the doctor insisted I wear. The doctors had originally told my parents I would be hospitalized a minimum of forty-nine days, and possibly as long as seventy-seven days. I was healed in fifteen days and discharged five days later.

I went to my church youth group meeting where I gave my testimony. Four days later, on a Sunday night, God's Spirit fell on our Baptist church. Adults were weeping; teenagers were weeping. Revival hit my church, which became the focal point of an even larger revival. During a span of forty-nine consecutive days, two hundred fifty people ranging in age from thirteen to twenty-three were saved. Eleven of us were called into ministry, including Mike Glenn, the county's biggest drug pusher, who was on the brink of suicide the night the Lord saved and delivered him. I will share more of his conversion story later.

The 250 people who were saved and healed and delivered during that revival (Mike included), along with the millions who have been saved worldwide down through the ages, give witness to the power of the cross to forgive us our sins, offer eternal salvation, deliver us from captivity and oppression, and heal us of diseases. The death of Jesus on the cross gives us so much more than a ticket to heaven. It is "the power of God unto salvation" (Rom. 1:16 KJV) given to us as spiritual gifts.

As we in the Christian church celebrate Communion (the Lord's Supper), much like our Jewish brothers and sisters who celebrate Passover, we are connecting to healing as a fulfillment of the prophecy of the prophet Isaiah given seven hundred years before it was fulfilled in Jesus. In Jesus Christ we find our glorious Savior, crucified and risen, who sits at the right hand of the Father to intercede for us and to be our advocate. His body and blood bring us all we need for life in this world here and now, and for eternal life with Him forever in heaven.

In answer to Pilate's question of why Jesus had to die, Scripture teaches that Jesus died to release the power and authority to heal.

three

JESUS DIED TO DESTROY DEATH

When I saw him, I fell at his feet as though dead. Then he placed
his right hand on me and said: "Do not be afraid. I am the First
and the Last. I am the Living One; I was dead, and now look, I am
alive for ever and ever! And I hold the keys of death and Hades."
—REVELATION 1:17–18

The crucifixion of Jesus destroyed the power of death, liberating His followers from the fear of death because if we believe in Him, we will never die, as He claimed in John 11:25–26: "I am the resurrection and the life. The one who believes in me will live, even though they die; and whoever lives by believing in me will never die. Do you believe this?"

Just as many other aspects of Jesus' crucifixion are portrayed in the Old Testament and fulfilled in the New Testament, so it is with His power over death. This is clearly illustrated in both 1 and 2 Kings where we find two instances of dead raisings through the prophets Elijah and Elisha.

These are the only two instances of the dead being raised found in the Old Testament.

OLD TESTAMENT DEAD RAISINGS

The first instance of a dead raising is found in the story of the widow Zarephath's son from 1 Kings 17.

> Now it came about after these things that the son of the woman, the mistress of the house, became sick; and his sickness was so severe that there was no breath left in him. So she said to Elijah, "What do I have to do with you, O man of God? You have come to me to bring my iniquity to remembrance and to put my son to death!" He said to her, "Give me your son." Then he took him from her bosom and carried him up to the upper room where he was living, and laid him on his own bed. He called to the LORD and said, "O LORD my God, have You also brought calamity to the widow with whom I am staying, by causing her son to die?" Then he stretched himself upon the child three times, and called to the LORD and said, "O LORD my God, I pray You, let this child's life return to him." The LORD heard the voice of Elijah, and the life of the child returned to him and he revived. Elijah took the child and brought him down from the upper room into the house and gave him to his mother; and Elijah said, "See, your son is alive." Then the woman said to Elijah, "Now I know that you are a man of God and that the word of the LORD in your mouth is truth." (vv. 17–24 NASB)

The second instance of a dead raising in the Old Testament is found in the story of the Shunammite woman's son from 2 Kings 4:18–37:

And the child grew. Now it happened one day that he went out to his father, to the reapers. And he said to his father, "My head, my head!" So he said to a servant, "Carry him to his mother." When he had taken him and brought him to his mother, he sat on her knees till noon, and then died. And she went up and laid him on the bed of the man of God, shut the door upon him, and went out.

Then she called to her husband, and said, "Please send me one of the young men and one of the donkeys, that I may run to the man of God [Elisha] and come back." . . .

When Elisha came into the house, there was the child, lying dead on his bed. He went in therefore, shut the door behind the two of them, and prayed to the LORD. And he went up and lay on the child, and put his mouth on his mouth, his eyes on his eyes, and his hands on his hands; and he stretched himself out on the child, and the flesh of the child became warm. He returned and walked back and forth in the house, and again went up and stretched himself out on him; then the child sneezed seven times, and the child opened his eyes. And he called Gehazi and said, "Call this Shunammite woman." So he called her. And when she came in to him, he said, "Pick up your son." So she went in, fell at his feet, and bowed to the ground; then she picked up her son and went out. (NKJV)

NEW TESTAMENT DEAD RAISINGS

Scripture records only three people raised from the dead by Jesus: Jairus's daughter, the widow of Nain's son, and Lazarus. However, in light of John 21:25, which says, "And there are also many other things that Jesus did, which if they were written one by one, I suppose that even the world itself could not contain the books that would be written" (NKJV), it is possible that Jesus raised more from the dead than the three.

In Old Testament accounts of dead raisings, God used prophets who prayed to the Lord to raise the dead. They had to rely on God's power as they had no power of their own. In contrast, when Jesus raised someone from the dead, He spoke and overcame the power of death, standing in the place of authority over death as the resurrection and the life (John 11:25–26).

Jairus's Daughter Raised from the Dead

In the instance of Jesus raising Jairus's daughter from the dead, Jesus was told that she was dying (Mark 5:23). As He began to make His way to the child, He stopped to heal a woman with an issue of blood. While He was ministering, word reached Him that the child had died (Mark 5:35–36). Knowing His authority over death, He continued to the home of Jairus to raise the child back to life.

> While [Jesus] spoke these things to them, behold, a ruler came and worshiped Him, saying, "My daughter has just died, but come and lay Your hand on her and she will live." So Jesus arose and followed him, and so did His disciples. . . .
>
> When Jesus came into the ruler's house, and saw the flute players and the noisy crowd wailing, He said to them, "Make room, for the girl is not dead, but sleeping." And they ridiculed Him. But when the crowd was put outside, He went in and took her by the hand, and the girl arose. And the report of this went out into all that land. (Matt. 9:18–19, 23–26 NKJV)

The Widow of Nain's Son Raised from the Dead

In the story of Jesus raising the widow of Nain's son from the dead, scripture notes that the mother of the dead child was the most grief-stricken. Not only had she lost a beloved child, but as a widow, she had lost her provider and protector. Jesus' response to her springs from His heart of compassion. Our Lord's concern for the suffering of others is displayed throughout Scripture and reflects the Father's heart for humankind.

> Now it happened, the day after, that He went into a city called Nain; and many of His disciples went with Him, and a large crowd. And when He came near the gate of the city, behold, a dead man was being carried out, the only son of his mother; and she was a widow. And a large crowd from the city was with her. When the Lord saw her, He had compassion on her and said to her, "Do not weep." Then He came and touched the open coffin, and those who carried him stood still. And He said, "Young man, I say to you, arise." So he who was dead sat up and began to speak. And He presented him to his mother.
>
> Then fear came upon all, and they glorified God, saying, "A great prophet has risen up among us"; and, "God has visited His people." And this report about Him went throughout all Judea and all the surrounding region. (Luke 7:11–17 NKJV)

Lazarus Raised from the Dead

The third person Scripture tells us that Jesus raised from the dead was Lazarus. This testimony is found in John 11:1–43. I have not included it here because it is such a lengthy passage. However, I urge you to read it. This was the miracle that brought the greatest opposition to Jesus, causing the religious leaders to plot to destroy His life and ministry (John 11:45–53). Unlike the other two dead raisings done by Jesus, where the person raised had been dead for a short time—probably no more than a few hours—Lazarus had been buried and dead for four days, making it impossible to dispute the miracle. As his sister said, "By this time there will be an odor" (John 11:39 ESV).

Parallels in the Gospels

In both the gospels of Mark and Luke we find parallels to the story of Jairus's daughter from the gospel of Matthew. Luke 8:42 tells us that the child was about twelve years of age. Verse 53 talks of the professional mourners who laughed at Jesus because they knew the child was dead. It is important to understand that professional mourners would have had much experience with death. In other words, they would know with certainty that Jairus's daughter was dead.

When Jesus found out that she had died, He took only Peter, James, and John with Him to the home of Jairus. Upon arriving, He encountered the professional mourners who were already mourning. In fact, they were making such a commotion that Jesus stopped and spoke to them before seeing the girl, asking why they were making such a ruckus since the girl was not dead, only sleeping. Their response was to laugh at Him, whereupon He promptly put them out of the house.

When Jesus entered the room with Peter, James, and John and the girls' parents, Mark 5:42 tells us that "immediately the girl got up and began walking . . . , and they were immediately overcome with amazement" (ESV). Luke 8:55 tells us: "And her spirit returned, and she got up at once" (ESV). Had she been alive when Jesus arrived, her spirit would not have already departed from her.

Raised Incorruptible

Jesus' resurrection was unique in that He alone never died again after His resurrection. He was raised incorruptible. He received a resurrection body, a glorified body. All of the other resurrections in the Bible were followed eventually by death. In Matthew 27:50–53, we find there were people raised from the dead at the time Jesus died, and after He was raised incorruptible these raised persons appeared to many people. "When Jesus had cried out again in a loud voice, he gave up his spirit. . . . and the tombs broke open. The bodies of many holy people who had died were raised to life. They came out of the tombs after Jesus' resurrection and went into the holy city and appeared to many people."

Other New Testament Dead Raisings

There are only three other recorded dead raisings in the New Testament, all in the book of Acts. Given the number of verified dead raisings in the church today, this is an interesting statistic. The first of the three dead raisings was that of Tabitha, or Dorcas (Acts 9).

> Now there was in Joppa a disciple named Tabitha, which, translated, means Dorcas. She was full of good works and acts of charity. In those days she became ill and died, and when they had washed her, they laid her in an upper room. Since Lydda was near Joppa, the disciples, hearing that Peter was there, sent two men to him, urging him, "Please come to us without delay." So Peter rose and went with them. And when he arrived, they took him to the upper room. All the widows stood beside him weeping and showing tunics and other garments that Dorcas made while she was with them. But Peter put them all outside, and knelt down and prayed; and turning to the body he said, "Tabitha, arise." And she opened her eyes, and when she saw Peter she sat up. And he gave her his hand and raised her up. Then, calling the saints and widows, he presented her alive. And it became known throughout all Joppa, and many believed in the Lord. (vv. 36–42 ESV)

The second dead raising in the book of Acts is related to Paul being stoned— many believed to death—and raised when his disciples stood around him:

> But Jews came from Antioch and Iconium, and having persuaded the crowds, they stoned Paul and dragged him out of the city, supposing

that he was dead. But when the disciples gathered about him, he rose up and entered the city, and on the next day he went on with Barnabas to Derbe. (Acts 14:19–20 ESV)

There are differing opinions as to what actually happened to Paul after this stoning. Some such as John Wesley point out that stoning to death was quite common in those days, and so those doing the stoning would have known how to kill a person in that way, and that an angry mob such as the one that surrounded Paul would have had no reason to hold back. Surely they would have finished him off before walking away. Yet Scripture teaches that he rose up when the disciples gathered about him, which would indicate that he was resurrected from the dead.

Others are of the opinion that Paul got up *after some time* and walked away because he wasn't dead. He just needed time to recover from the stoning, which could have been classified as a miracle healing but not a dead raising. I agree with John Wesley. I believe the disciples raised Paul from the dead in the power of the Holy Spirit.

The third dead raising is found in Acts 20. If you recall, Paul raised Eutychus, who fell from a third-story window.

Seated in a window was a young man named Eutychus, who was sinking into a deep sleep as Paul talked on and on. When he was sound asleep, he fell to the ground from the third story and was picked up dead. Paul went down, threw himself on the young man and put his arms around him. "Don't be alarmed," he said. "He's alive!" Then he went upstairs again and broke bread and ate. After talking until daylight, he left. The people took the young man home alive and were greatly comforted. (vv. 9–12)

I agree with those commentators who believe that the man died, because Scripture says he was "picked up dead." When Paul first took him in his arms, the young man was dead, but God raised him, and Paul reassured the people that "his life is in him."

Power and Authority for Believers

Jesus not only has power over death, He gives that power and authority to His followers to see the dead raised as well. This power is given through the Holy Spirit so that those who follow Jesus, and are part of His church, can be used to do even greater things than Jesus did. That is what Jesus said in John 14:12: "Very truly I tell you, whoever believes in me will do the works I have been doing, and they will do even greater things than these, because I am going to the Father."

We know from John 14:13–16 (the Upper Room discourse) that Jesus died so that the Holy Spirit—who is the true source of miracles, healings, deliverance, and dead raisings done in the name of Jesus by His followers—could be poured out.

When Jesus commissioned the Twelve in Matthew 10:8, He instructed them to "Heal the sick, raise the dead, cleanse those who have leprosy, drive out demons. Freely you have received; freely give." This commission is for all believers, for all time until Jesus returns in glory. The Great Commission (Matt. 28:18–20) must be read in light of the commissioning of the Twelve, as well as the seventy-two Jesus sent out in Luke 10.

Now, let us turn our attention to what God is doing in our time around the world, beginning with the United States.

DEAD RAISINGS IN THE UNITED STATES

What we are seeing in the United States and around the world is evidence of believers today walking in the Matthew 10:8 commission. The following testimonies are from people I either know personally or have personally interviewed.

Dead Man Raised

Let's begin with a testimony from my cardiologist, Chauncey Crandall IV, MD.

Jeff Markin walked into the hospital emergency room and died. As the chief cardiologist I was called to the scene. I went to the emergency room and walked in, and there was a man who had a massive heart attack. They'd been working on this man for more than thirty minutes, and he was dead. The doctor running the case came in and said, "What do you think we can do?" I said, "That man is dead, there is nothing you can do." Or so I thought . . .

This was a morning that I was very busy and didn't even want to go to the emergency room, but the staff had asked me into the situation. This man was clinically dead. I was the cardiologist in the hospital for the day, so they wanted another opinion on whether they'd done all the protocol to bring him back to life. I had to sign off on him being dead and get on with my work.

I had never seen anyone this dead before. Amazingly, his whole body was black. We call it cyanosis. We finished the code, and the emergency room doctor declared him dead. They were cleaning the body and preparing it for the morgue. Everyone had left the room except for me and a nurse.

I started to leave the room when I heard the Lord speak to me. He said, "Turn around and pray for that man." I didn't listen to it the first time. I kept walking because I didn't want to stay. The Lord said again, "Turn around and pray for that man." After the second time I walked to the side of the stretcher and prayed over that man.

I prayed audibly, quietly. The nurse was on the other side of the stretcher. The arms were draped over the side. There was no breathing, of course. He was covered up. The nurse had been pulling all the tubing out of the body preparing it for the morgue, sponging the body down.

I said, "Lord, what am I going to pray for this man? What do I pray for him?" The Holy Spirit took over, and all of a sudden these words came out of my mouth: "Father God, I cry out for this man's soul. If he does not know you as Lord and Savior, raise him from the dead now in Jesus' name."

I was praying for this man but had no control of my words really. It was the power of the Holy Spirit taking over the prayer. The nurse looked at me like I was crazy. All of the sudden, his right arm shot up in the air. The emergency room doctor walked in, and I said, "Shock this man one more time." He said, "No, he's dead. We've declared him gone." I said, "Shock him one more time," and he did so out of respect for me, to show me the man was gone. He took the paddles, put them on the chest, and immediately a perfect heartbeat came back on the monitor. I had never seen that before in all my training, all my years going back to Connecticut and Duke University.

I was stunned. I looked at the monitor; the emergency room doctor and nurse looked at the monitor. We couldn't believe what was happening. Then all of the sudden his chest started moving with air. Then the hand started moving, then the leg started moving. The nurse screamed, "Dr. Crandall, what will we do with him now? What have you done?" I said, "I cried out for his soul."

The nurse thought he was brain dead but we rushed him down to the intensive care unit. The other nurses were all talking about this case. We arrived in the intensive care unit and I put him in his bed. It was late on a Friday night, and I signed this case out to my partner. I said, "I'm signing you out a dead man who was raised from the dead in the name of Jesus. Nothing you can do this weekend will hurt him because he has a call on his life."

I came in on Monday, and the man was sitting up in bed fully alert, looking at me, talking. I said, "What happened to you that day?" He said, "I'm so disappointed. I was in total darkness. I was in a casket in a dark room, and I was there for eternity and no one came to visit me. My family didn't come, my relatives, my colleagues didn't come to visit me. After being there for eternity, these men came in and wrapped me up and threw me in the trash."

I said, "Jeff, never again do you have to be thrown in the trash if you accept Jesus as your Lord and Savior." I reached out and grabbed his hand, we prayed the sinner's prayer, and he accepted the Lord right there in the hospital bed with tears running down his face. I said, "Today is the day of salvation. You are free in Christ."[1]

Dead Boy Raised

This next story was told to me several times by Nancy, who has been on several of our mission trips and has received training from our ministry.

Nancy and her husband were having a holiday with their family at the lake. Their grandson was on a Jet Ski at the lake when he had an accident. He ran into a boat and suffered massive injuries that killed him instantly. It took some time for his father and another friend to reach the boy. When they arrived back at the dock with the boy's body, a doctor checked the teenager and pronounced him dead.

Nancy, the boy's grandmother and one of our partners in ministry, knelt down beside the boy, placed her hand on his chest, and began praying for him to come back to life, speaking life into his body. After praying that way several times, the grandmother said, "Johnny, this is your grandmother, I command you to come back into your body!" At that moment the boy came back to life. He has since graduated from college.

Cure the Sick, Raise the Dead, Cleanse the Lepers, Cast Out Demons

This next testimony I want to share with you was in part the result of a sermon I preached. But before I preached that sermon, God had to do some work in me. It began in the late 1990s when I was called to preach for my friend Cleddie Keith in his church in Florence, Kentucky. My message was on the biblical basis for healing. As I sat reviewing my notes and going over scripture, I came to the commissioning of the Twelve in Matthew 10:7–8: "As you go, proclaim the good news, 'The kingdom of heaven has come near.' Cure the sick, raise the dead, cleanse the lepers, cast out demons" (NRSV). That one phrase "raise the dead" had always bothered me.

Then the Holy Spirit spoke to my heart through a strong impression. He said, "You don't like that scripture, do you?" I replied, "No, Lord, I don't. That scripture is an embarrassment to the church. You are telling us to raise the dead while we are trying to get the sick healed. I wish You had left out the dead raising."

What came next was a quick and quite strong rebuke from the Holy Spirit. I heard, "Don't you dare become an experience-based preacher who only preaches what you have experienced! Don't you dare lower My Word to the level of your experience! You preach My Word and let your experience rise to My Word, but don't lower My Word to your experience."

I was shocked by this impression. It seemed to be a play on the accusation made by dispensational cessationists who do not believe the gifts are still for today; that Pentecostals and Charismatics are experience-based preachers who don't preach the Word of God—the Bible. At the time I only knew of two testimonies of people who had been raised from the dead. I felt the Holy Spirit impress upon me that if we don't preach about dead raising and share the testimonies, there will be no faith built for dead raisings.

I finished preparing my sermon on the biblical basis for healing, and when I stood up to preach it, I preached and emphasized dead raisings and that they are still happening today. Then I shared the two testimonies I had heard from Argentinian evangelist Omar Cabrera, whom God had used to raise two people from the dead. A few years later, I met the young man who had been playing lead guitar on the worship team the day I preached in Cleddie Keith's church. He shared with me the story of his son's resurrection.

It happened as he was walking through his house one day and looked out the window. Seeing a lot of people gathered in the street, he was hit with fear, thinking something had happened to his young son. Running out the front door, he saw his son's tricycle lying bent on the ground. In the street lay his little boy. As a trained EMT working for an ambulance service, he knew the signs of death and his son had them all—no pulse, dilated unmoving eyes, and no respiration.

At first he cried out in agony and grief. Then, remembering the message I had preached about dead raising, he began calling for his son to come back into his body, commanding him by name to come back. After a few minutes of commanding him to come back, the boy gasped for air and began to cry. He had been raised from the dead! Not only that, but the many bones that were broken when the car hit him healed in a fraction of the time it normally would have taken for bones to heal.

I Didn't Believe in Miracles, but Now I Do

As I was writing this chapter on dead raisings, I spoke about raising the dead and my work on this book while preaching at a church. Afterward, an American named Aaron Simmons shared with me that he has been involved in several dead raisings because of his work as a fireman. Time and space don't permit me to share all his testimonies, so one will have to suffice. Here is what Aaron wrote:

My partner and I had been in administration at the fire department for a while. We were in charge of fire prevention and inspections. Needless to say, because it had been a while since we ran call, our paramedic skills were rusty. The medic at the station house where our prevention division was housed had just responded to a medical call. Moments later we received another call to a doctor's office directly across the street. A man was in cardiac arrest and not breathing.

My partner and I insecurely looked at one another and said, "Well, we should probably go help." We grabbed an outdated first-aid bag, with who knows what in it since we rarely assisted with calls like that anymore. We walked across the street and met a nurse at the front door and she took us to the back. The family physician was with the elderly man who had collapsed in the office. The man was lying on his back and the physician had already placed a heart monitor on him. The monitor was showing an asystole rhythm (a flat-line rhythm indicating no electrical activity within the heart).

Upon initial assessment, the man was apneic (not breathing) and pulseless. He was mottled, pale, and his pupils were fixed. An indescribable blue-purple-black color began to flow from his core and fill his extremities and his head. I asked the physician and staff if this man had a "do not resuscitate" order. They informed me that he did. They then provided proof of the official document. Due to our policies and guidelines, we were not allowed to initiate any care or resuscitative efforts. The physician confirmed time of death. I radioed to the ambulance that was in route to this emergency that they could cancel and not respond due to a field termination.

The staff informed me that the gentleman's wife was waiting in the lobby. I also operate as our department chaplain, which most often means I am the guy to meet and console family members when there is a death. I went into the lobby and met with his wife. I let her know that her husband had passed away and that we honored their wishes to not resuscitate him. She thanked me and said she understood. We briefly embraced and I told her if she needed anything to let me know. I asked her to give us a moment to take him off the heart monitor and then she could come back to see him.

As I walked back into the back offices from the lobby, I realized that I hadn't prayed or even asked God to raise him from the dead. Since the Bible basically promises seventy years, and eighty if a person is righteous, I have a funny way of how I approach raising the dead. If they are under seventy, no matter what, it's an injustice, and since God is loving and just, I demand life. If they are seventy to eighty years old, I ask the Lord to raise them. If they are over eighty, I simply ask for His will, and for Him to do as He wishes.

As I approached the man, they were taking off the wires of the heart monitor and placing a sheet over his body. By this time, I would estimate it was twenty to thirty minutes since we were initially called. In a gentle way and in an effort to say I had at least tried, I reached out my hand to his head and began to say, "In Jesus' name . . ."

Well, by the time I got the name "Jesus" out, he took the largest gasp of air I have ever seen. The indescribable blue-purple-black color began to flush out of his body the opposite way it filled him, and just as fast. The man looked up at me and said, "I'm uncomfortable. Can you get me a pillow?" My eyes were as big as the staff's, and my partner was looking at me with absolute amazement. We were all shocked!

Of course I gave him a pillow. Then, I immediately radioed back to the ambulance we had previously cancelled and requested for them to respond again to transport him to the hospital. I went back into the lobby where his wife was patiently waiting. I was still in shock and hadn't really rehearsed how to tell her this, so I just went for it.

I said, "I'm not sure what you believe, but something incredible just happened. I went back to your husband and prayed for him and he came back to life."

Her response was just as fun as the miraculous event that had occurred. She simply said, "Oh yeah. I believe in that." I then took her back to her husband where they briefly talked and held hands until the ambulance arrived to transport him to the local hospital for evaluation. My partner and I stumbled around trying to tell the paramedic crew what happened as we transferred care to them.

Now for my favorite part of the story . . .

I wasn't sure what the other paramedics or hospital staff would say, think, or believe. I wasn't exactly sure how I was going to explain all of this. I especially didn't want them to think I was some freak. But miracles have a way of speaking for themselves. My partner, who happened to be the social butterfly of the department and an influencer, began to shout from the rooftops exactly what happened.

He told the entire story to all the nurses, paramedics, and crews from other departments who happened to be at the hospital. He even called his wife from his cell phone. He began to nearly yell things like, "I didn't believe in miracles, but now I do!" Then he said, "Aaron is like Peter; people are literally healed in his shadow!" He elaborated that in his twenty-three-year career, he had never seen anything like that.

That man walked out of the hospital on his own with no deficits. The hospital did not find anything at all wrong with him. It's still a fun story that my partner and others share today around the department.

DEAD RAISINGS AROUND THE WORLD

As amazing as the dead-raising stories from the United States are, they are not confined to America. Dead raisings are happening all over the world. Let me share a few of them with you.

Brazil

In Uberlandia, Brazil, a city in the south of the country, a young teenage girl was healed after being prayed for. She received her normal sight back—she had been seeing double for several weeks. And, she was able to walk without her wheelchair as well. What was even more exciting was the rest of her testimony. She had been raised from the dead a few weeks earlier after being dead for somewhere between thirty minutes and an hour.

On the day she died, she left the church to cross the street with her mother who was walking behind her. Partway across the street she dropped her pencil, and when she bent down to pick it up, she was hit by a motorcycle and killed instantly. The impact sent her flying in the air. She landed on the concrete curb of the road and cracked her skull open, exposing her brain. Her arm was broken as well. Her mother witnessed the accident.

The mother ran to her daughter and began praying for her to be raised from the dead. Several minutes later the emergency vehicles arrived. They checked the girl and told her mother she was dead, that it was too late for prayer; the child had already died. But the mother would not be dissuaded from praying. She prayed to the point where she was frustrating the men who wanted to take her daughter's body to the morgue. Realizing she had reached a crisis point, she grabbed her cell phone and called her group leader in her church to come help pray. By that time approximately half an hour had transpired since the accident. As both the mother and her friend prayed, the girl came back to life.

When our ministry team arrived eight days later and prayed for her, her eyes were healed and she was able to walk again. The girl told us that when she died everything went black and then she was in a beautiful white place. Jesus came to her and told her that He was sending her back because her mother and another woman wouldn't give up on her.

CHILD ON LIFE SUPPORT

During this same series of meetings in Uberlandia, we learned of another dead raising. A six- or seven-year-old girl who wore leg braces was healed when a couple of laymen on my team obeyed the leading of the Holy Spirit to take her leg braces off. She had not been able to walk without the braces. When they took them off she began to walk, even run across and around the stage. The mother came to me and wanted to tell me the rest of the story.

I had come to the city about six or seven years earlier for the first time. On that trip, this girl's mother had come from the hospital with a picture of her newborn baby asking me to pray for the child. I didn't like praying for pictures when there were so many people to pray for who were present. However, Brazilians have a lot of faith for healing, even utilizing pictures, so I prayed. I must admit that the faith in this story wasn't mine; it was the mother's. I simply prayed a short prayer, which was easier than explaining why I didn't want to pray for pictures. The mother had neglected to tell me that the baby had died and was on life support. After I prayed for the baby, the mother returned to the hospital to find the baby had been restored to life. And there she was, several years later, running around the stage at our meeting with her legs healed.

Needless to say, this experience changed my attitude about praying for people in pictures. There are many more stories about dead raisings in Brazil that space does not permit me to share here.

Kenya

Years ago I spoke at Elim Bible Institute and College in New York state. As part of the Pentecostal stream of the church, Elim trains and equips Spirit-filled believers. This particular event was the annual meeting of their pastors. While there, I met a distinguished older gentleman who turned out to be the former president of the college. When I meet people who have had the opportunity to have lots of interesting experiences, I usually ask them to share some of the most powerful experiences with me.

This man proceeded to tell me about a missionary who had been sent out to Kenya during the Latter Rain revival, through prophecy. He had moved his entire family there. Though he had labored there for some time (I think several weeks or months), he was not successful in reaching people for Christ.

One day while in the city he prayed, "Lord, You sent us here. I have moved my entire family to Kenya in obedience to Your prophetic word. But, Lord, nothing is happening. No one is being saved, or healed, or delivered. Lord, You have to do something! If You don't move, I will fail." As he was praying, the answer came. "Go to that funeral procession coming down the street," he heard the Lord say, "and tell them you are to raise the man from the dead."

He obeyed, went to the funeral procession, laid hands on the coffin, and prayed for the man to come back to life. Within seconds thuds could be heard from inside the coffin. The man inside had been raised from the dead and he was pounding on the lid to be let out! Revival broke out as a result of this dead raising, with ten thousand new churches established in Kenya through this one missionary group.

Mozambique

During one of my visits to Mozambique, I had the privilege of interviewing Mozambican pastor Tanueque through a translator. I was very interested to hear his testimonies about raising people from the dead. What follows are three of his testimonies of dead raisings.

TESTIMONY 1

A child died. The family was not near their home and so I, as local pastor, made my house available. The family brought the dead child into our house. As the family gathered there, my wife and I asked for permission to pray for the child. We had faith to say, "The peace of the Lord be in this house." With the family's permission, my wife and I picked up the child and started to pray. When we saw the child begin to move, we had great faith to continue to pray. Then the child's eyes opened. The family was crying, but I told them not to scream or cry but to be quiet. They were quiet and the child was 100 percent raised from the dead. The child is alive to this day. We do not know how long the child had been dead, but the length of time we prayed was thirty minutes before the child was raised from the dead.

TESTIMONY 2

I passed by a house and heard people screaming and crying. When I asked what was happening, they told me a child had died. When I went inside the house, I saw that they had covered the child with a sheet. I removed the sheet and prayed for the child. Then God gave me the courage to pray for the child to be raised up to life. With this courage, I started to pray and believe. I cried out and the child rose from the dead.

TESTIMONY 3

There was a lady who came and said her child had died. I went to the house because when I hear people have died, I want to go. When I got there, I started to pray for this child. Immediately the child started shaking. The child was six years old. The child then moved and came back to life. I brought the mother, father, and child to a conference with Heidi and said that this was the child who had been raised from the dead.

JOHNNY'S FIRST DEAD RAISING

During the time of my first trip to work with Rolland and Heidi Baker and their ministry Iris Global in Mozambique, they had only been able to establish a few hundred churches. I believe only a couple of dead raisings had occurred by that time. Today there have been a multitude of dead raisings in Mozambique alone through their ministry, and more than ten thousand churches planted.

The first pastor and key leader of the movement to raise the dead was a man named Johnny. Several years earlier I had given a prophecy to Heidi Baker, when she was visiting the Toronto Airport Vineyard Church. The prophecy was, "Heidi, do you want the nation of Mozambique?" "Yes!" she tearfully replied. Then I said, "God is going to give you the nation of Mozambique. You will witness the blind see, the deaf hear, the lame walk, and the dead be raised." Immediately the power of God hit Heidi, causing her to shake, sweat, weep, laugh, feel peace, and hear the audible voice of God. He told her to gather twelve men together, and when she asked them to join her in her ministry they would. God even showed Heidi the faces of the twelve men. When Heidi asked the men to join her, they all did.

Then the Holy Spirit told Heidi she was to "prophesy to these men everything that Randy just prophesied to you." When she prayed for them and prophesied over them, the Lord showed her the two men He would use to raise the first people in Mozambique from the dead. She told those two men to begin to pray for the dead—that they were going to raise the dead. Johnny was one of these two men.

Mozambican pastor Supresa Sithole took me to see Johnny, to interview him about this one and only dead raising at the time. We sat down in two white plastic chairs outside, and I began the interview with Johnny.

Johnny told me the person he had raised from the dead was a woman. She had become sick from disease and then died. Johnny heard of her death and went to pray for her. He laid hands on her and commanded her to come back to life. She did and told him she was hungry, so he prepared some food for her.

"Johnny," I said, "I believe your testimony, but I am from 'Nazareth,' from the United States where there is so much skepticism and doubt about the miraculous. For the sake of the people of my country who are so skeptical, I need to ask you this question. Since there were no doctors involved [she died at home, as most do in Mozambique, many miles away from the nearest doctor], how do you know for sure she was dead?" He replied, "She didn't have a pulse, there was no breath, her eyes were fixed and glazed, and she was cold and was becoming stiff."

"I think even skeptical North Americans would agree this is evidence she was dead," I said. Then I asked him, "Do you believe you will raise others from the dead?" He laughed and said, "Of course!" He was correct; God has raised others from the dead through Johnny.

SUPRESA SITHOLE: HOW TO RAISE THE DEAD

At the time of this writing, Supresa has raised at least eight people from the dead. Here is his testimony of his first experience of raising someone from the dead.

The first time that I experienced it [raising the dead], I didn't know that people really could rise from the dead. I was in this village, and we started revival meetings. It was me and a young man, George. The people came there, and it was about fifty to seventy people who came on that Monday. I preached, then on Tuesday the number dropped to maybe twenty people. On Wednesday morning the chief said I had to stop my crusade because in the place where we were doing the crusade someone died. Because of the death, we would have to come back another time.

I asked to go to the house to offer my condolences. When I arrived there, I found six ladies sitting inside. The chief introduced me to them, and then he went to his house. I asked the ladies if I could pray, and they gave me permission. I started praying, and after praying for quite some time, I was just feeling myself [get] very comfortable. When I opened my eyes, I found all the ladies were sleeping. I had prayed a long time. When I saw that, it gave me the opportunity to go closer to the dead body and start unwrapping the dead body. If they had been awake, they would not have let me unwrap the body.

Suddenly, a hand came out and I put my finger on the hand. It was cold and stiff and couldn't bend or move. I prayed and worshiped the Lord, when suddenly—I really didn't know what was going on— the formerly dead girl grabbed my finger, causing me to jump and scream. This happened as I was unwrapping the body. The hand was the only thing unwrapped; the rest of the body was still wrapped. I was completely shocked. Then the girl said, "I'm hungry."

The mother was still sleeping. I believe God has a sense of humor. He did not want me to tell the women to go out while I stayed there to pray. "Don't worry, Supresa," I heard God say. "Just let them stay where they are, sleeping."

There was a two-liter bottle of Coca-Cola nearby. I opened it and gave it to the girl, then I woke up the mother. The mother jumped up and ran outside screaming and cheering. The chief heard the noise and came to the house and asked what was happening. I explained to the chief, and then I asked if I could continue the crusade. That night there was a massive crowd as a result of the dead raising, and many people came to faith in Jesus. This is typical of the fruit of someone being raised from the dead.

One week later, Pastor Johnny prayed for somebody who rose from the dead. That same week, another pastor prayed and there was a dead raising. One miracle, one dead raising, is a catalyst. Once that happens other Christians and leaders realize that if God can do it for me, He can do it for them.

If you would like to learn more about what God is doing in Mozambique and elsewhere regarding dead raisings, watch the Sid Roth video interview of Supresa Sithole that aired November 23, 2019. You can find his testimonies and more in his book *Faith to Raise from the Dead*.

In answer to Pilate's question of why Jesus had to die, Scripture teaches that Jesus died to destroy death.

four

JESUS DIED TO DISARM AND TRIUMPH OVER THE POWERS AND AUTHORITIES

When you were dead in your sins and in the uncircumcision of your flesh, God made you alive with Christ. He forgave us all our sins, having canceled the charge of our legal indebtedness, which stood against us and condemned us; he has taken it away, nailing it to the cross. And having disarmed the powers and authorities, he made a public spectacle of them, triumphing over them by the cross.

—COLOSSIANS 2:13–15

This passage from Colossians is one of my favorites because it says much about the benefits of Christ's death. However, for purposes of this chapter, I want to focus on verse 15: "And having disarmed the powers and authorities, he made a public spectacle of them, triumphing over them by the cross."

The New King James Version translates the Greek words for "powers and authorities"—*archas* and *exousias*—as "principalities and powers." Some commentators believe this is a reference to worldly governmental and religious powers, but the better and more ancient understanding is that this is a reference to two of the levels of the demonic hierarchy (cf. Rom. 8:38–39; 1 Cor. 15:24; Eph. 1:21; 2:2; 6:12; Heb. 2:14; and 1 Peter 3:22). These verses further support the perspective that the powers and authorities or the principalities and powers represent not human government but demonic powers.

Colossians 2:15 is a frame of reference, a lens through which we see one perspective of the reason Jesus died, a perspective related to the Christus Victor theory of atonement. Jesus Christ is victor over the powers and authorities and over the devil and his demonic hierarchy. The cross of Christ is a place of victory. God took the initiative to reconcile us, to redeem us, and He used the cross to do it. In the incarnation of the Word—the life, death, and resurrection of Jesus—God turned His face toward the world to redeem us to life, overcoming the power of sin, death, and the devil, thereby setting us free. He "rescued us from the domain of darkness, and transferred us to the kingdom of His beloved Son, in whom we have redemption, the forgiveness of sins" (Col. 1:13–14 NASB).

SPIRITUAL AUTHORITY, PRAYER, AND SPIRITUAL WARFARE

Spiritual authority, prayer, and spiritual warfare became important in my life in the mid-1990s. The issue was not the traditional sense of spiritual warfare with the focus on personal deliverance. Instead, the focus was on praying against powers and principalities to bind or dislodge them for a period of time so more successful evangelism could occur.

I traveled to Argentina to investigate for myself how this was being done, who was doing it, and what the precautions were. I met with Omar Cabrera, one of the most well-known pastors at that time, because of his expertise in strategic level spiritual warfare (SLSW). In addition, I met with Carlos Annacondia; Pablo Bottari, who was Annacondia's trainer for the deliverance tent; Gerimo Preim; Gorge Marcus of Montevideo, Uruguay; Harold Caballeros of Guatemala City, Guatemala; the pastor of the largest Baptist church in Brazil with fifty thousand members; Abe Huber of Brazil, whose church would grow to more than seventy thousand in Santerém, Brazil; and many others. I spent much time discussing views on SLSW with these key leaders. The question was whether or not this practice was biblical.

Soon after my time in Argentina, John Paul Jackson published his book *Needless Casualties of War*, which carried a strong warning on the dangers associated with praying against powers and principalities. Then I discovered C. Peter Wagner's book on SLSW that took the practice and made it a model intended to be homogenous among those practicing SLSW. The model in Wagner's book did not accurately reflect the practices I found in Latin America, where there were a variety of understandings, viewpoints, and practices regarding SLSW, ranging from being open with anyone doing SLSW, to only those called and anointed, or a select group of the church who were consecrated, mature believers.

Those in the first group, who practiced SLSW, believed Colossians 2:15 provided the basis to minister in this way. Others believed that while casting out demons from people was biblical, there was no biblical evidence or basis for SLSW. Neither time nor space will allow for me to share what I learned in Latin America about SLSW. I have hours of interviews but have not yet felt released to write a book on what I learned. For now, one story must suffice.

Omar Cabrera is the most famous person associated with SLSW that

I have been privileged to meet. In the course of many conversations, he shared how he came to be engaged in this particular ministry. He had spent many days in a hotel room praying, worshiping, and studying the Bible, when a demon appeared in his room in a physical form that he could see with his physical eyes. This demon told Cabrera that he (the demon) could "take care of a person" who had been causing Omar grief. Omar understood that "taking care of the person" meant that the demon would kill them.

Repulsed by the idea, Omar refused to give permission to the demon. However, the reality of the demon caused Omar to have great faith in the reality of holy angels and their willingness to help Christians on earth. His belief was strengthened by the passage in Revelation where the angel tells John not to bow in front of him because he is a fellow servant with those who hold to the testimony of Jesus.

Omar went on to tell me that in his times of prayer and worship over a city before a crusade, there would sometimes be moments of breakthrough when he felt permission from God to address the powers and principalities with the authority to bind them from exercising their power over the city for a matter of days. When this happened, he felt confident to spend scores of thousands of dollars on the crusade knowing that the *strong man* (the name Jesus uses for the devil in Matthew 12:29) had been bound for a time. With the strong man bound, blinders would fall from the eyes of those attending the crusade, making them much more open to receiving Christ. When this happened, instead of hundreds being converted, thousands would come to Christ, with many more healings and miracles.

When Omar didn't experience the breakthrough moment, he chose not to spend the money in mass advertising in the city because he had learned from experience that unless the blinders were removed from the eyes of the people, the numbers of healings and miracles would be much less, as well as the number who were converted. For him and many of the other pastors in Argentina, engaging in SLSW was not out of the question. They understood the power of the cross to triumph over principalities and powers and were confident to engage when they sensed permission from God. Others did not believe they had to have a breakthrough to come against the powers and authorities and principalities.

JESUS BROUGHT US BOTH A SOCIAL AND PERSONAL GOSPEL

It is not unusual today to see powerful social programs as part of Pentecostal-Charismatic churches due to the fact that they are often large churches with thousands of members and have greater resources to serve the community. Why is this happening around the world today? Because Jesus went to the cross identifying with the people who needed the power of God to break the stronghold that the authorities, powers, and principalities held in their lives and often over their lives.

As Pilate tried to "wash his hands" of the crucifixion of Jesus, he could not have imagined that in less than 300 years Christianity would become a legalized religion in the empire, or that approximately 350 years after he participated in the crucifixion of Jesus, the Roman Empire would make Christianity its official religion. He couldn't have imagined when his soldiers were mocking Jesus, slapping Him, spitting on Him, and placing a crown of thorns on His head that there would come a day when there would be no Roman Empire and that the followers of Jesus would number more than one billion.

In answer to Pilate's question of why Jesus had to die, Scripture teaches that Jesus died to disarm the powers and authorities, making a public spectacle of them, triumphing over them by the cross.

five

JESUS DIED SO THAT HE MIGHT RANSOM PEOPLE

Historically there has been much discussion among theologians as to how God accomplished what He accomplished on the cross. Different theories have emerged and taken hold, dominating the landscape of the church for a time before giving way to something new. Today, several atonement theories exist and different factions of the church embrace them according to how they interpret Scripture. Together we will briefly examine some of the major atonement theories, as time and space do not permit a more thorough examination. Let's begin with the ransom theory of atonement.

THE RANSOM THEORY OF ATONEMENT

According to the ransom theory, with the fall of Adam and Eve in the garden, all humanity came under the sentence of death and under the dominion of the god of this world (the devil) and the elemental spirits (demons) that executed the deception of the devil. Due to Adam and Eve's sin in the garden, humanity's fall from righteousness left us mired in sin, iniquity, and transgressions. As defeated sinners, we became slaves to Satan and his demons, living in the darkness of deceit, helpless and trapped. For justice to be accomplished, the devil's right to the souls of humankind (his slaves) was paid by the soul of our Savior, Jesus Christ. Jesus, the Righteous One, established our righteousness, saving us from the slavery of the devil. The death of our souls was defeated by the One who destroyed death. Ransom theology dominated the first one thousand years or so of church history, finding support in the Greek church fathers.

Jesus accomplished this act of ransom by living as a sinless human and dying on the cross. His death bound the devil, giving authority for us to plunder the devil's house in the authority of the name of Jesus. The obedience of Christ unto death reversed the disobedience of Adam and Eve. Some of the metaphors early theologians used to explain the ransom theory were so objectionable that they caused a reaction against it. For instance, Christian scholar Origen of Alexandria (AD 184–254) used the analogy of a fishhook upon which Jesus was the bait to illustrate the ransom theory. Theologian Augustine of Hippo portrayed Jesus as cheese in a mousetrap as bait for the devil. They positioned Jesus Himself as the ransom, with His life paid in death *to Satan* for the freedom of those held captive by the devil, both in life and in death. However, on the cross, Satan was deceived and defeated by God. Jesus rose from the dead and took captivity (humanity) captive, delivering us from death and damnation once and for all.

THE SATISFACTION THEORY OF ATONEMENT

Anselm of Canterbury, in his satisfaction theory, argued that the ransom was not paid to the devil, for God cannot be in debt to the devil. Rather, he proposed that the ransom Jesus paid on the cross was paid to God the Father to satisfy His honor, because our sin had taken away the honor God was due. The death of Jesus as fully God and fully man was sufficient to cover the dishonor of humankind's sin. This is why the Savior had to be both human and divine—why God became a human while at the same time retaining His deity—a mere man's death would not suffice to cover the dishonor of all of humankind's sin.

Psalm 49:7–8 says, "Truly no man can ransom another, or give to God the price of his life, for the ransom of their life is costly and can never suffice" (ESV). In other words, it is impossible for one person to ransom another. That is why there had to be the God-Man—Jesus—to ransom us from our predicament, our alienation, our degradation, our state of being under the sentence of death. Anselm's satisfaction theory eventually gained popularity and became the dominant theory in the Roman Catholic Church. It was embraced by the Protestant Church when it emerged, as well as the Eastern Orthodox Church, for about five hundred years until it gave sway to the penal substitutionary understanding of the cross, which was an adaptation of satisfaction theology and was held by the Protestant churches, especially the Calvinists.

THE PENAL SUBSTITUTIONARY THEORY OF ATONEMENT

Penal substitutionary atonement says that Jesus died on the cross as our substitute—a substitute for sinners. This was possible because God imputed (assigned) the full weight (guilt) of our sins to Jesus, our vicarious substitute, who bore the punishment for us. The cross served as full payment for sin, thereby satisfying both the righteousness and the wrath of God. In this way, God is able to forgive us without compromising His holiness. The penal substitution theory serves to set us free from the penal demands of the law—our sins that are punishable by law—thereby satisfying both the righteousness of the law and the holiness of God. It became the predominant understanding of the cross for Evangelical Protestants.

CHRISTUS VICTOR

In 1931 Gustaf Aulén, bishop in the Church of Sweden, published *Christus Victor: An Historical Study of the Three Main Types of the Idea of Atonement.*[1] His analysis of the doctrine of atonement reintroduced what he termed the "classic" theory of atonement as understood by the early church fathers as well as Scripture. The central theme of *Christus Victor* is the resurrection. It is in the resurrection of the incarnate Christ that we see the fullness of the lordship of Jesus who divinely rescues humankind from the bondage of sin, death, and the devil, liberating us for all time. It is in this final act of resurrection that God reconciles the world to Himself. *Christus Victor* sees the atonement as divine conflict and victory, with the suffering and death of Jesus on the cross triumphing over the powers and authorities holding humanity in the bondage of sin. In this triumph of God in Christ, we (humankind) are re-created. Athanasius of Alexandria was well known for saying: "He became what we are so that he might make us what he is."

OUR NEED FOR REDEMPTION

The Bible makes clear our need for redemption, a term closely related to ransom—that is, a price paid to set free those in bondage to another. The following scriptures reveal the need for redemption or liberation and utilize the language of ransom.

"[J]ust as the Son of Man did not come to be served, but to serve, and to give his life as a ransom for many." (Matt. 20:28)

"For even the Son of Man did not come to be served, but to serve, and to give his life as a ransom for many." (Mark 10:45)

"For there is one God and one mediator between God and mankind, the man Christ Jesus, who gave himself as a ransom for all people. This has now been witnessed to at the proper time." (1 Tim. 2:5–6)

"For this reason Christ is the mediator of a new covenant, that those who are called may receive the promised eternal inheritance—now that he has died as a ransom to set them free from the sins committed under the first covenant." (Heb. 9:15)

WARFARE AND THE POWER OF GOD

One thing is certain: the Bible is clear that Jesus came to ransom a people for God. Again, the question is, "To whom did He pay the ransom—the devil or the Father?" Or was it that the means of bringing about our release from the power of the devil was not so much by a payment to the devil as it was the cost of defeating the devil? Let me try to illustrate what I am saying. When American soldiers or civilians are taken captive by an enemy, there are two ways a ransom can be obtained—through negotiation or attack. Negotiation is an attempt to reach a settlement and pay to the captors what they want. Payment can be money where the term "ransom" is often connected to a kidnapping. Or, it could be a prisoner exchange where the enemy releases the captive(s) in exchange for some of their captives being returned.

Another way a price is paid is through an attack on the enemy's location where the captives are being held. One could think of an American SEAL team going in to overcome enemy forces and rescuing the captives. If there was loss of life among the SEAL team, we would typically hear something along the lines of, "We paid a great price to set the captives free." And in truth, blood was shed and life was given to set captives free. However, the price that was paid was not paid to the enemy. It wasn't a negotiation. The ransom paid was in the form of a battle with the enemy, a costly battle. The loss of life wasn't paid to the enemy, and neither was it paid to the American government. The ransom paid was the cost of war, of conflict, of rescuing captives from their captors. The loss of life was the necessary price to pay in order to overcome the enemy's forces and set captives free.

The ransom theory of atonement was an attempt to understand the verses of the Bible that use the word *ransom* in regard to Jesus paying the price to set people free—the price Jesus paid to take captivity captive. Originally, this metaphor was not focused on the satisfaction or the penal substitution understandings of the cross. It was focused on the warfare and the power of God to destroy the power of the enemy. Satisfaction theology began in the eleventh century, and the penal substitution theory came into the church in the sixteenth century. Early on in the church's understanding of ransom theology, the graphic metaphors being put forth by theologians became quite strategic as a hidden wisdom of God, with Jesus the bait on a hook offered to the devil who believes God is vulnerable by taking on flesh as fully man in Jesus. To this way of thinking, the devil bites the bait, killing Jesus while not realizing that He is not merely a man, but also fully God, who has resurrection power.

Jesus, able to die in His humanity, enters the realm of death. Once in the kingdom of darkness, the devil, who since the garden of Eden has held the keys to death and Hades, is defeated by the resurrection power of

Jesus. However, the resurrection power of Jesus is not mere resurrection like Lazarus and others experienced. It is much greater. The resurrection power of Jesus is glorification where death can no longer touch those raised. Sown in weakness and raised in power; sown in dishonor and raised in honor; sown corruptible and raised incorruptible, the glorious resurrection power of Jesus defeats the enemy of death. Using metaphorical language, Jesus takes the keys to death and Hades from the devil.

THE MYSTERIES OF GOD

Modern-day theologian Gregory Boyd believes this metaphor can only be pushed so far. However, he proposes that it did try to explain not only the scripture verses on ransom but also a verse that became part of the illustration of the fishhook and the bait: "None of the rulers of this age understood it, for if they had, they would not have crucified the Lord of glory" (1 Cor. 2:8).[2] This verse is referring to the wisdom of God that is revealed through the preaching of the cross (1 Cor. 2:6–7).

In context, what is being referred to that was not understood by the rulers of this age is the "mystery of God." The demons and the demonical hierarchy understood the weakness of the cross—its apparent repulsiveness to both Greek and Jew. They knew that Jesus was the Son of God, the Holy One of God. They even knew that He had come to destroy them. Yet, they did not know or understand that the means of their destruction would be the cross, that God would use the crucified Savior to destroy the power of Satan. That was the mystery, as was the inclusion of the Gentiles—that God would open the door of the covenant people of God to the Gentiles, not just the Jews.

Another aspect of the mystery was the coming Pentecost, the new covenant reality of the power of God via the Holy Spirit coming upon

God's people. This power would enable them to experience, in this life as well as the life to come, the glory of God (Col. 1:25–29). This glory has often been restricted in Protestant thought to the glorification of our resurrection bodies at the end of the Age, reducing the power of Paul's statement regarding the "glorious riches of this mystery, which is Christ in you, the hope of glory," to the future millennial or end of age context.

When one considers that the number one way God glorifies His name in the Bible is through what He does and the testimonies of what He does, then this verse has a present application as well. The anointing of the anointed one via the Holy Spirit causes the hope of God's power to be manifested through those who believe in Jesus Christ. The result is that God's glory can be manifested to the world and to the powers and principalities in the heavenly realms by believers here and now and in the future. A choice between future glory and present glory is not required; both are true.

THE WISDOM OF GOD REVEALED IN THE CROSS

His Spirit in us is our assurance of ultimate salvation, with glorification of our bodies, and is also the hope of being used by the Holy Spirit, in the gifts of the Spirit, to bring glory to God by our good news in word and deed. "This, the first of his signs, Jesus did at Cana in Galilee, and manifested his glory. And his disciples believed in him" (John 2:11 ESV). It is the wisdom of God revealed in the cross of Christ. The rulers of this age (the demonic), and the actual Jewish and Roman rulers, did not know that crucifying Jesus at the instigation of the demonic rulers was about to bring about salvation as liberation from death, disease, and the demonic power to keep us bound in sin. It is through the delivery and demonstration of the gospel that the

Church fulfills God's plan to make His wisdom known even to the kingdom of darkness, where those who have rebelled against God (and fallen from heaven) reside.

"His intent was that now, through the church, the manifold wisdom of God should be made known to the rulers and authorities in the heavenly realms" (Eph. 3:10). This revelation of God's manifold wisdom was not and is not to be limited to the proclamation of the gospel in words. God also makes His manifold wisdom known by deeds done by the power of the Holy Spirit.

In Romans 15:17–19, Paul gives voice to the early church's understanding of how they were to proclaim and verify the gospel, which was to bring the gospel through word *and* deeds done by the power of the Holy Spirit with signs and wonders, healing, and miracles.

> Therefore I glory in Christ Jesus in my service to God. I will not venture to speak of anything except what Christ has accomplished through me in leading the Gentiles to obey God by what I have *said and done—by the power of signs and wonders, through the power of the Spirit of God.* So from Jerusalem all the way around to Illyricum, I have fully proclaimed the gospel of Christ. (emphasis mine)

It is interesting to note that the word *proclaimed* in verse 19 is not in the original Greek manuscripts. Instead, Paul was referencing the healings and deliverances throughout the region that had become the verification of the gospel that the kingdom of God is at hand. Paul had filled up the area from Jerusalem to Illyricum—modern-day Albania—with the demonstrations of the power of God. Indeed, the gospel of Christ had been "proclaimed" as modern translations say, but Paul's emphasis is not only proclamation but demonstration of God's power to cause people to believe the gospel.

Christianizing the Roman Empire is a wonderful book that reveals that

Europe was Christianized by demonstrations of the power of God. The primary causes were two: first, deliverance through the name and power of Jesus' name, and second, healing done in His name, usually associated with the preaching of the gospel. As Jon Ruthven stated, "In the New Testament, however, the revelation of God in miracles doesn't 'prove' the Gospel—it expresses the Gospel."[3]

SALVATION IS ROOTED IN THE PROCLAMATION OF THE GOOD NEWS

I want to turn our attention for a moment to some of the references to ransom found in the Old Testament. For the purposes of this book, let's begin in the book of Hosea. "I shall ransom them from the power of Sheol; I shall redeem them from Death. O Death, where are your plagues? O Sheol, where is your sting? Compassion is hidden from my eyes" (Hos. 13:14 ESV).

Now, let's look at how the apostle Paul, in his first letter to the Corinthians, saw this Old Testament passage fulfilled.

> Behold! I tell you a mystery. We shall not all sleep, but we shall all be changed, in a moment, in the twinkling of an eye, at the last trumpet. For the trumpet will sound, and the dead will be raised imperishable, and we shall be changed. For this perishable body must put on the imperishable, and this mortal body must put on immortality. When the perishable puts on the imperishable, and the mortal puts on immortality, then shall come to pass the saying that is written: "Death is swallowed up in victory." . . .
>
> The sting of death is sin, and the power of sin is the law. But thanks be to God, who gives us the victory through our Lord Jesus Christ. (1 Cor. 15:51–54, 56–57 ESV)

Sheol was the place of the dead and was closely associated with death. In Jesus, the fulfillment of the hope of Hosea is realized. Death has been defeated! These Old Testament verses in Hosea, taken together with these New Testament verses in 1 Corinthians, are a wonderful counterbalance to keep the church from going into the heresy of universalism, the belief that all humankind will eventually be saved. Matthew and Mark both state that Jesus gave Himself as a ransom for many (Matt. 20:28; Mark 10:45).

In 1 Timothy 2:6, Paul wrote, "[Jesus] gave himself as a ransom for all people." This verse indicates that there is a general atonement—that Jesus died that all could be saved. However, all are not saved, but many are saved. Salvation is rooted in the proclamation of the good news. People are lost in their sins, captives to their demonic captors, deceived by the devil—the father of lies—living as slaves to their sins in the kingdom of darkness. The gospel is the power of God unto salvation, able to rescue those who are perishing. The good news (of the gospel) is that the devil's power has been broken, the *strong man has been bound*, and his house is being plundered and his possessions are being carried off (Matt. 12:29).

This passage in Matthew is a metaphor for the mission of Jesus, and as a metaphor, certain aspects aren't to be taken literally. For example, Jesus is not praising stealing, but pointing to the reality that to raid the devil's domain, to destroy death, to take captivity captive in order to set the captives free, you first have to bind the strong man. That is what the cross did—it bound the power of Satan. This is what was accomplished by the ransom that Christ paid. Again, this ransom was not paid to the devil. That is where the metaphors or illustrations of the fishhook and the mousetrap break down.

Here one has to ask, "Why was the incarnation necessary?" The incarnation was necessary to give Jesus a body through which He would be able to: 1) reveal Himself (and I would add—reveal the Father); 2) defeat death, and to do this He would have to defeat the power of the devil;

and 3) restore life. This "life" is not mortal life, but immortality. Athanasius did not believe immortality was a natural condition of the human soul, but rather a gift from God to those who had relationship through faith with Him in Christ. Athanasius stated in Volume 4:

> And thus taking from our bodies one of like nature, because all were under the penalty of the corruption of death he gave it over to death in the stead of all, and offered it to the Father—doing this, moreover, of his loving-kindness, to the end that, firstly, all being held to have died in him, the law involving the ruin of men might be undone (inasmuch as its power was fully spent in the Lord's body, and had no longer holding-ground against men, his peers), and that secondly, whereas men had turned towards corruption, he might turn them again towards incorruption, and quicken them from death by the appropriation of his body, and by the grace of the Resurrection, banishing death from them like straw from the fire.[4]

WALK IN NEW LIFE

There is some truth in all the Church's understandings of the atonement. However, some are more central or carry more weight than others, such as Christus Victor. We need them all to gain the fullest understanding. These perspectives are complementary, not contradictory, perspectives or understandings of the cross and are not meant to be held in tension against each other. The Bible speaks of righteousness as being able to live rightly by the power of God. It involves the beginning of salvation—imputed righteousness through which we have the boldness to come to the throne of grace in our time of need so that we can experience the grace and the enabling power of God to break us free of the sins that hinder and hurt us.

Justification is the entry door to the kingdom of God through which we have grace to grow and throw off lifestyle behaviors that are destructive to us. I believe in the *finished work of Christ*. He is my *hagiasmos*, my sanctification.[5] We must follow our liberator out of captivity, out of the region of the enemy in order to experience the freedom for which Jesus paid the ultimate price. The strong man has been defeated. Get up and out of prison. Leave the darkness and walk into the light. The pending death sentence has been broken. Walk in the new life!

In answer to Pilate's question of why Jesus had to die, Scripture says that Jesus died in order that He might ransom people.

JESUS DIED SO WE COULD BE BAPTIZED *IN*, *WITH*, AND *BY* THE HOLY SPIRIT

All four Gospels recognize Jesus as the one who baptizes with the Holy Spirit. Just as God used the Jewish feasts of Passover and the Day of Atonement to respectively point to Jesus as the deliverer and the healer, and our great High Priest, as well as the sacrificial goat and the scapegoat, God uses the Feast of Tabernacles to point to Jesus as the Baptizer in the Holy Spirit.

> On the last day of the feast, the great day, Jesus stood up and cried out, "If anyone thirsts, let him come to me and drink. Whoever believes in me, as the Scripture has said, 'Out of his heart will flow rivers of living water.'" Now this he said about the Spirit, whom those who believed in him were to receive, for as yet the Spirit had not been given, because Jesus was not yet glorified. (John 7:37–39 ESV)

Before the outpouring of the Holy Spirit on the day of Pentecost could occur, there had to be the crucifixion, resurrection, and ascension. Jesus had to take His place in heaven as our intercessor, our great High Priest. And, having inaugurated the new covenant in His blood, He could then begin His work as the Baptizer in the Holy Spirit.

THE CROSS BRINGS THE HELPER

Jesus' self-understanding connected the necessity of the cross to the outpouring of the Holy Spirit. His words from the Upper Room discourse indicate this truth:

> Nevertheless, I tell you the truth: it is to your advantage that I go away, for if I do not go away, the Helper will not come to you. But if I go, I will send him to you. And when he comes, he will convict the world concerning sin and righteousness and judgment: concerning sin, because they do not believe in me; concerning righteousness, because I go to the Father, and you will see me no longer; concerning judgment, because the ruler of this world is judged. (John 16:7–11 ESV)

Even prior to this moment in the discourse, Jesus had already spoken of the outpouring of the Spirit:

> If you love me, keep my commands. And I will ask the Father, and he will give you another advocate to help you and be with you forever—the Spirit of truth. The world cannot accept him, because it neither sees him nor knows him. But you know him, for he lives with you and will be in you. I will not leave you as orphans; I will come to you. Before long, the world will not see me anymore, but you will see me. Because I live, you also will live. On that day you will realize that I am in my Father, and you are in me, and I am in you . . . But the Advocate, the Holy Spirit,

whom the Father will send in my name, will teach you all things and will remind you of everything I have said to you. (John 14:15–20, 26)

THE PROMISE OF THE FATHER: THE HOLY SPIRIT

Luke is considered by biblical scholars to be the "theologian of the Holy Spirit." No other gospel writer speaks as much about the Holy Spirit as Luke does. Both his gospel and its sequel, the book of Acts, emphasize the Holy Spirit, and Jesus' emphasis upon the Spirit as the promise of the Father. Two passages in particular are most important for us:

I am going to send you what my Father has promised; but stay in the city until you have been clothed with power from on high. (Luke 24:49)

But you will receive power when the Holy Spirit comes on you; and you will be my witnesses in Jerusalem, and in all Judea and Samaria, and to the ends of the earth. (Acts 1:8)

However, before Jesus made these statements—the first from the Upper Room on the night before He was crucified, and the second just before His ascension—He used the Feast of Tabernacles to bring two great truths about Himself to the people's attention. One would deal with water (John 7), and the other with light (John 8). Approximately six months separate the Feast of Tabernacles and the Feast of Passover.

At the end of the first day of the Feast of Tabernacles, also known as Sukkot, four great candelabras were lit, each with four branches that would hold ten gallons of oil. These candelabras were fifty-five feet in height and located in the temple. The temple was on the highest hill in the city, which meant the "illumination of the temple" could be seen from all over the city.

The Feast of Tabernacles was to be a time of rejoicing for seven days, celebrated with joy and with plenty to eat and drink. The "drawing of the waters" was a ceremony in which the priests went to the Pool of Siloam to draw water with two golden pitchers, one filled with wine, and the other with water drawn from the well to be taken to the temple and poured out. J. B. Lightfoot, in his commentary on John 7:37–39, quoted Rabbi Judah as saying, "Whoever hath not seen the rejoicing that was upon the drawing of this water, hath never seen any rejoicing at all."[1] There were flute players and dancers to contribute to the joyous occasion. Many believed it was this joyous scene that Jesus was drawing upon that is recorded in John 7.

I find it interesting that the Feast of Tabernacles pointed to the out-pouring of the Holy Spirit, which would be made possible after Jesus was glorified through the crucifixion, at the time of Passover, and the resur-rection and ascension. It is also interesting that of all the feasts, this one in particular is the one that emphasizes joyous celebration. This glorification that John spoke of in verse 39 would result in Jesus pouring out the Holy Spirit fifty days after Passover, on Pentecost. There the disciples would be accused of being drunk, perhaps because of the great joy the Holy Spirit brought to them.

EMPOWERED BY THE SPIRIT

The day after the Day of Illumination spoken of in John 7, Jesus, as He spoke to the people, would draw upon the theme of light, which was also associated with the Feast of Tabernacles. He was in the temple courts when He said, "I am the light of the world. Whoever follows me will never walk in darkness, but will have the light of life" (John 8:12).

The Holy Spirit is the source of joy typified in the Feast of Tabernacles. He is the One who enlightens people to the truth about God and themselves.

He is the light of truth, the light of life. Jesus identified Himself as the light of the world. Since His resurrection and ascension, the Holy Spirit has continued this light-giving ministry of Jesus to this very day.

I was taught by my mentor, Dr. Jon Ruthven from United Theological Seminary, that it was possible to preach the Bible every Sunday and not emphasize what the Bible emphasizes, even possible to never speak on the emphasis of the Bible. And that is why he said that we as ministers should be intentional to emphasize what the Bible emphasizes. What is this emphasis? Jesus' main purpose with His disciples was to empower them by baptizing them with the Holy Spirit and to commission them to carry on His ministry of proclaiming the kingdom of God just as He had during His three years of ministry. The empowering of the Holy Spirit would enable them to do what Jesus had been doing, which was healing and delivering people from disease and demons while preaching the message of the kingdom of God.

THE JOY OF THE LORD IS OUR STRENGTH

Recently I was talking with a professor of religion at an Ivy League school who had been experiencing visitations of the Holy Spirit that would cause his body to tremble all over. These visitations would occur at various times, including when he was preparing for his classes or writing his latest book. I asked him if he knew of other professors of religion who were having visitations of the Holy Spirit, and he said he did.

One such testimony is that of another professor of religion, who likewise had a PhD, but had no experience with Charismatics[2] or Pentecostals. He would be sitting at his office desk studying when all of a sudden he would break out in hilarious laughter. This professor said that he did not know why this was happening to him. Nothing funny was going on, no one had shared anything humorous, and he was not even having a humorous thought. It was spontaneous joy. I believe God wants us to know that the Holy Spirit is a joy bringer. Of the three characteristics of the Holy Spirit—love, joy, and peace—joy is second only to love.

From the mid-1990s till this day, I have been associated with a movement of the Holy Spirit that was characterized so much by laughter that it was called the "Laughing Revival." Why should we be shocked by such joy? The typology of Tabernacles should help us to be open to such joy, such celebration, even laughter.

The baptism in the Holy Spirit enables us to more powerfully, boldly, and effectively communicate the gospel to others through word and deed, by the power of signs and wonders, in the power of the Spirit. Jesus died to make it possible for His followers to not only be born of the Spirit, baptized into the body of Christ by the Spirit, and sealed by the Spirit, but also to experience the promise of the Father—the baptism in and by and of the Holy Spirit.

As of October 2019, I have been in ministry forty-nine years. During this time of ministry, which I hope will continue for another twenty years, I have thus far been baptized in the Spirit by Jesus three times. The first time was in 1984, the second time in 1989, and the third time in 1993. These are three of the most important experiences of my soon-to-be sixty-eight years of life. Only the birth of my children and my marriage to DeAnne compare with these experiences.

In each of these instances, I experienced different things: electricity, heat, power, love, tears, joy, laughter, peace, falling to the ground, and contortions in my hands and body. There was even a time when the power of God flowing through my body was so strong I began to fear I would literally die if it were to increase even just a little bit. I have written in detail about these experiences, as well as the experiences of others, from both a biblical perspective and a Christian historical perspective as it relates to baptism in the Spirit, in five books.[3]

To answer Pilot's question at the trial of Jesus, "Why? What crime has He committed [that would merit crucifixion]?" here is part of the answer. Jesus was crucified so He could become the Baptizer in the Holy Spirit. We would first be baptized by the Holy Spirit into the body of Christ, then Jesus would baptize us in the Holy Spirit to give us power to minister in the kingdom of God. The first baptism is for eternal life; the second is for power to minister in this life.

seven

JESUS DIED TO BECOME THE MEDIATOR OF THE NEW COVENANT

For there is one God, and there is one mediator between God and men, the man Christ Jesus . . .
—1 TIMOTHY 2:5 ESV

Scripture tells us that Jesus Christ is the one mediator between us and God. Yet, why is this so? How is Jesus unique in His ability to fulfill this role of mediator so utterly and completely? First, let's be clear on what the writers of Scripture mean when they use the word *mediator*. The Greek for "mediator" is *mesitēs*, and is defined as "a go-between, an internunciator, or (by implication) a reconciler (intercessor):—mediator"; "one who intervenes between two, either in order to make or restore peace and friendship, or form a compact, or a ratifying covenant; a medium of communication, arbitrator."[1]

With this definition in mind, it follows that the one who fulfills this role of mediator between God and men has to be able to relate fully to both parties. Otherwise he would be biased in one direction or the other, or unable to fully appreciate both. Because Jesus was both fully God and fully man, He alone is able to represent both parties with justice and holiness.

JESUS: FULLY GOD AND FULLY MAN

Let's dig into this a little more, beginning with a brief examination of the two natures of Jesus. First, the two natures of Jesus Christ are distinct—He is one person with two natures that make up His substance. One nature was not grafted into the other, nor does the divine nature of Christ change into our human nature. The two natures do not mix. They exist in Christ as distinct. Yet, there is but one Jesus. It is precisely because of these two natures that Jesus perfectly fulfills the role of the one mediator between God and men. He can perfectly represent both of us—God and man—with the fullness of the new covenant.

So, how is Jesus able to perfectly represent us? The writer of Hebrews tells us, "For we do not have a high priest who is unable to empathize with our weaknesses, but we have one [Jesus Christ] who has been tempted in every way, just as we are—yet he did not sin" (Heb. 4:15). Jesus isn't just feeling compassion for us in our weakness. He experienced our weaknesses and yet remained without sin. As He mediates on our behalf, as He intercedes for us with the Father, He does so with an understanding that comes from His fully human nature. On the cross, His flesh experienced every temptation known to man. The one who was pierced for our transgression, crushed for our iniquities, the one who took the punishment that brought us peace, the one by whose stripes we are healed (Isa. 53:5 NKJV) is Jesus. The New Living Translation says, "He was beaten so we could be whole. He was whipped so we could be healed."

Jesus, our mediator, "having abolished in his flesh the enmity"

(Eph. 2:15 NASB) between sinful humans and God, made peace so that we might be reconciled once more to God. This reconciliation took place on the cross, and we enter into it as members of the new covenant. God's new covenant with believers is His promise to humankind that He will forgive us our sins and, through Jesus Christ, restore us to fellowship when we put our faith in Christ alone as Savior and redeemer.

The prophet Jeremiah predicted this new covenant:

> "Behold, the days are coming, declares the LORD, when I will make a new covenant with the house of Israel and the house of Judah, not like the covenant that I made with their fathers on the day when I took them by the hand to bring them out of the land of Egypt, my covenant that they broke, though I was their husband, declares the LORD. For this is the covenant that I will make with the house of Israel after those days, declares the LORD: I will put my law within them, and I will write it on their hearts. And I will be their God, and they shall be my people. . . . for they shall all know me, from the least of them to the greatest, declares the LORD. For I will forgive their iniquity, and I will remember their sin no more." (Jer. 31:31–34 ESV)

Notice that several aspects of the new covenant appear in this passage: true holiness that springs from the indwelling of the Holy Spirit as we receive a new heart and a new spirit. God's original promise to Israel was the new covenant.

BETTER PROMISES

In Hebrews 8:6, the writer speaks of "better promises" when referencing the new covenant: "But in fact the ministry Jesus has received is as superior to theirs as the covenant of which he is mediator is superior to the old one, since the new covenant is established on better promises."

What does the writer of Hebrews mean in this passage? What are these "better promises"?

One answer is found in the difference between the old covenant temple and our new covenant temple. The old covenant temple was a foreshadowing of what was to come—a physical place where high priests performed their duties. As we know, these duties—the continual sacrifice of sheep and goats to atone for the sins of the people—was inferior to the sacrifice of Christ on the cross. Jesus is our perfect sacrifice. He is our great High Priest after the order of Melchizedek. The better promises of God in Jesus took place in God's heavenly temple, not in an earthly temple. And because of the finished work of the cross, believers—you and I—have become the temple of the living God, who dwells in us as "Christ in [us], the hope of glory" (Col. 1:27).

A second answer is found in God's remedy for our sin nature. Jeremiah speaks of the Israelites breaking God's (old) covenant after He brought them out of captivity. Why did they break it? They broke it because the blood of sheep and goats was not sufficient to once and for all atone for their sins. They circumcised their flesh when it was their hearts that needed circumcision. No matter how many animals were sacrificed by the high priests in the temple, the people were not able to keep God's commandments (the Law) in their own power. They needed the empowerment of God working in them that was released to all believers on the cross. It is the blood of Jesus, who is our new covenant, that has the power to defeat sin and death.

The prophet Ezekiel spoke of the "new heart and . . . new spirit" God would put within His people (Ezek. 36:26). This heart transformation is possible only because of the power of God's Spirit working in us, drawing us to Him in a love-centered relationship that fills our hearts with a desire to do God's will. This Spirit became available to us through the cross, and continues to be available to all believers until the triumphant return of Christ.

Jesus Himself is the new covenant, which was established by him personally—in His flesh that was impacted with such terrible brutality as to make Him unrecognizable on the cross. Jesus established this new covenant with His blood, and now we can enter in by faith in Him because of the power of His resurrection, and because of His unending intercession (mediation) for us. It is precisely where sin abounds that the power of the cross can be seen most clearly.

NOT THE BLOOD OF SHEEP AND GOATS

In his letter to the Hebrews, the writer explained the significance of the difference between the blood of Old Testament (old covenant) sacrifices and the blood of Jesus:

> But you have come to Mount Zion and to the city of the living God, the heavenly Jerusalem, and to innumerable angels in festal gathering, and to the assembly of the firstborn who are enrolled in heaven, and to God, the judge of all, and to the spirits of the righteous made perfect, and to Jesus, the mediator of a new covenant, and to the sprinkled blood that speaks a better word than the blood of Abel. (Heb. 12:22–24 esv)

Renowned scholar and theologian Craig Keener wrote that in this passage, the writer of Hebrews "merely felt that animal sacrifices were inadequate for human redemption in the heavenly sanctuary" (9:23), and thus unnecessary now that Christ had come.[2] We know that Moses is considered the mediator of the old covenant. Under that covenant, Abel's blood spoke condemnation, crying out to be avenged. There had to be a "better blood" for a new covenant. In order to inaugurate this new covenant, there had to be a shedding of blood that brought the forgiveness of God—speaking a better word.

The blood of Jesus is unique in that it comes from the one who is both fully God and fully man. The humanity of Christ united with the divinity of God in Jesus gives us the only blood that could mediate the new covenant. We have been given a great gift in the cross of Christ. Yet, many never turn to Jesus and embrace what He freely gives. Sixteenth-century theologian William Whitaker, in *The Mediator of the Covenant Described in His Person, Nature, and Offices*, wrote, "In rejecting this Mediator, you sin against the highest and greatest mercy that ever was vouchsafed to creatures."[3] He went on to implore us to receive Jesus in all His offices—as our Mediator, our High Priest, our Redeemer, our King, "our great prophet while on earth . . . revealing by his Word and Spirit the will of God for the salvation of his people,"[4] and the one who baptizes with fire and the Holy Spirit. Because as Jesus said in John 6:53, "Very truly I tell you, unless you eat the flesh of the Son of Man and drink his blood, you have no life in you."

THE FULLNESS OF THE NEW COVENANT

The new covenant mediated by Jesus was inaugurated on the cross, and continues to unfold today in the power of His Spirit. It is this baptism of the Spirit that empowers us to live a new covenant life. It is the power of the Spirit that renews our minds to conform them more and more to the mind of Christ. The progressive work of sanctification occurs by the power of the Spirit of God working in us. Jesus died and left this earth in order that we might receive this precious Holy Spirit. After His resurrection, Jesus appeared to His disciples and spoke to them, telling them to wait for the baptism of the Spirit to be poured out on them with power for the work He was commissioning them to do.

> Then he opened their minds to understand the scriptures, and he said
> to them, . . . "I am sending upon you what my Father promised; so stay
> here in the city until you have been clothed with power from on high."
> (Luke 24:45–46, 49 NRSV)

So many in the church today have missed this empowerment of the Spirit promised by God and spoken of by Jesus. My good friend and mentor, theologian John Ruthven, wrote about this in my book *Baptized in the Spirit*.[5] I urge you to read it. It is one thing to embrace the Father and the Son, but without the third person of the Trinity—the Holy Spirit—the gospel is truncated. Without the Holy Spirit, the Christian life is two-dimensional. When John the Baptist proclaimed Jesus Christ, he said that there was one coming after him who was more powerful than him, one who would baptize with the Holy Spirit and fire (Matt. 3:11–12).

God has given us a three-dimensional kingdom where Father, Son, and Holy Spirit are accessible. Yet, many today settle for a life void of the empowerment of the Spirit. Jesus died so that we might be baptized with the Spirit. He promised us the Holy Spirit and told us to wait for it before going into the world with His great commission (Luke 24:49). Why should we not receive all that He has to give us?

> And I will ask the Father, and he will give you another Advocate, to be
> with you forever. This is the Spirit of truth, whom the world cannot
> receive, because it neither sees him nor knows him. You know him,
> because he abides with you, and he will be in you. (John 14:16–17 NRSV)

But I tell you the truth, it is for your benefit that I am going away. Unless I go away, the Advocate will not come to you; but if I go, I will send Him to you. And when He comes, He will convict the world in regard to sin and righteousness and judgment. (John 16:7–8 BSB)

In answer to Pilate's question of why Jesus had to die, Scripture says that Jesus died to mediate the new covenant. God's new covenant—His promise to humankind that He will forgive us our sins and, through Jesus Christ, restore us to fellowship when we put our faith in Christ alone as Savior and Redeemer—is a magnificent gift given to us by God the Father and Jesus the Son, and sealed with His blood on the cross. Thanks be to God—Jesus Christ our great mediator now sits at the right hand of the Father, forever reconciling us to God and making all things new and forevermore pouring forth His Holy Spirit, who comes from the Father through the Son to baptize us in His power.

May the God of peace, who through the blood of the eternal covenant brought back from the dead our Lord Jesus, that great Shepherd of the sheep, equip you with everything good for doing his will, and may he work in us what is pleasing to him, through Jesus Christ, to whom be glory for ever and ever. Amen. (Heb. 13:20–21)

eight

JESUS DIED TO BECOME OUR GREAT HIGH PRIEST

Nor did he [Jesus] enter heaven to offer himself again and again, the way the high priest enters the Most Holy Place every year with blood that is not his own. Otherwise Christ would have had to suffer many times since the creation of the world. But he has appeared once for all at the culmination of the ages to do away with sin by the sacrifice of himself. Just as people are destined to die once, and after that to face judgment, so Christ was sacrificed once to take away the sins of many; and he will appear a second time, not to bear sin, but to bring salvation to those who are waiting for him.

—HEBREWS 9:25–28

Frank Stagg, Baptist professor of New Testament Interpretation and Greek, in his book *New Testament Theology,* noted the following regarding the high priesthood of Jesus Christ that is reflected in the book of Hebrews.

Jesus as High Priest is after the order of Melchizedek (Heb. 5:10; 6:20). Melchizedek was not a Jew and was not of the lineage of Aaron and the Levites (7:4–17); his priesthood was eternal and unchanging (7:1,3,22–25); it was one of continuing intercession, providing salvation to the uttermost to all who come to God through Jesus (7:25); as High Priest Jesus was also referred to as mediator (8:6; 9:15; 12:24); he offers up himself in sacrifice (7:27; 9:14); he writes his laws upon our hearts and minds (10:16) which is a New Covenant reference.[1]

In Old Testament Jewish temple life, the high priest's primary function was to present persons before God (2:17). Another function was to bring many sons into glory (2:10). This was made possible by the high priest's animal sacrifices and intercession through which he expiated (atoned) for the sins and propitiated (satisfied) the wrath against sin, overcoming the sins of the people (2:17).

Under the new covenant, Jesus, our great High Priest, identifies with us as our brother (2:11) while breaking the power of sin and death for us (2:14) through His sacrifice on the cross. The death of Jesus is understood and explained by the apostle Paul as being revelation, reconciliation, redemption, and righteousness.[2] In 1 Corinthians 1:31, Paul quoted from the prophet Jeremiah: "But let him who boasts boast in this, that he understands and knows me, that I am the LORD who practices steadfast love, justice, and righteousness in the earth. For in these things I delight, declares the LORD" (Jer. 9:24 ESV).

This passage from Jeremiah was read by the temple high priest on the Day of Atonement as he entered into the Holy of Holies to offer a sacrifice for his own sins and the sins of the people. As a Jew who grew up studying the Torah, Paul understood the fullness of the identity of Jesus as our great

High Priest: "It is because of him [God] that you are in Christ Jesus, who has become for us wisdom from God—that is, our righteousness, holiness and redemption. Therefore, as it is written: 'Let the one who boasts boast in the Lord'" (1 Cor. 1:30–31).

While it is important to note that Jesus, as the High Priest who offers Himself as the sacrifice to take away our sins, in so doing propitiates (satisfies) the wrath of God, the new covenant focus isn't on the wrath of God, but on the grace of God. "But we see Jesus, who was made a little lower than the angels, now crowned with glory and honor because He suffered death, so that by the grace of God He might taste death for everyone" (Heb. 2:9 BSB).

Many biblical commentators believe the book of Hebrews was written just months before the fall of the temple in AD 70 and consider it to be the most profound interpretation of the death of Jesus in the New Testament. Baptist theologian Dale Moody divides Hebrews into two sections. Section one, chapters 1–7, pertains to the office of Jesus as the High Priest. Section two, chapters 8–13, pertains to the sacrifice of Jesus. Moody also identifies four "betters" in chapters 8 through 13. He says Jesus brings:

1. A better priesthood (8:1–5).
2. A better covenant (8:6–13).
3. A better sacrifice (9:1–10, 18).
4. A better promise (chapters 11–13).[3]

The sacrifice of Jesus as well as His role as our great High Priest are both "better" types than their Old Testament counterparts.

Let's look at the other functions or roles that Jesus fulfills as our great High Priest as found in Scripture.

THE FORERUNNER AND THE AUTHOR AND PERFECTER OF OUR FAITH

As High Priest, Jesus has the apostolic role of being the forerunner or the author of our salvation and faith (Mal. 3:1; Mark 9:37; Luke 10:16; and John 12:44). For first-century Jews, the word *apostle* had the meaning of "one sent by another." It was also associated with the leader on the lead ship of an armada, or the general who was going to establish a Roman colony and city. In his apostolic role, Jesus was the *One* sent by the Father to establish on earth the atmosphere and culture of heaven.

OUR SYMPATHETIC HIGH PRIEST

Jesus, our sympathetic High Priest, is able to sympathize with our sins because He Himself was tempted in every way yet was without sin. Because of this, we can come before Him with confidence when we need the empowerment of the Holy Spirit in the midst of temptations.

> For we do not have a high priest who is unable to sympathize with our weaknesses, but we have one who in every respect has been tested as we are, yet without sin. Let us therefore approach the throne of grace with boldness, so that we may receive mercy and find grace to help in time of need. (Heb. 4:15–16 NRSV)

THE AUTHOR OF OUR SALVATION

Salvation comes through Christ alone. There is no other way to be delivered and protected from the dangers and death of sin except through the redemptive work of God in Jesus on the cross.

Although he was a Son, he learned obedience through what he suffered; and having been made perfect, he became the source of eternal salvation for all who obey him, having been designated by God a high priest according to the order of Melchizedek. (Heb. 5:8–10 NRSV)

THE ONE WHO TAKES US INTO THE PRESENCE OF GOD

The death of Jesus on the cross takes us within the veil into the very presence of God. If you recall, the Jews in Old Testament days could not directly approach God. A thick curtain veiled the entrance to the Holy of Holies in the temple, and only the high priest could go beyond that veil into the presence of almighty God. Jesus not only provides us access to God; He has gone before us as the forerunner, into the Holy of Holies (Heb. 6:19) as an example of how we can live in the power of God.

THE FINISHER OF OUR FAITH

The writer of Hebrews gives us the example of Jesus as the finisher of our faith. In other words, there is nothing we can do to improve upon what Jesus accomplished on the cross to increase our faith. Faith is a gift that has been given to us by Jesus, to embrace in this life as a member of the great cloud of witnesses.

Therefore, since we are surrounded by so great a cloud of witnesses, let us also lay aside every weight and the sin that clings so closely, and let us run with perseverance the race that is set before us, looking to Jesus the pioneer and perfecter of our faith, who for the sake of the joy that was set before him endured the cross, disregarding its shame, and has taken his seat at the right hand of the throne of God. (Heb. 12:1–2 NRSV)

It is this gift of faith that makes us as believers perfect or complete in Him through the creative work He does in us, joining us to Him in such a real way that our response is to give ourselves to God in faith, expressed in obedience.

OUR MEDIATOR, THE ONE WHO INTERCEDES ON OUR BEHALF

Associated with the concept of a high priest who intercedes and makes sacrifice on our behalf for our sins is that of the *paraklētos* of 1 John 2:1–2:

My dear children, I write this to you so that you will not sin. But if anybody does sin, we have an advocate with the Father—Jesus Christ, the Righteous One. He is the atoning sacrifice for our sins, and not only for ours but also for the sins of the whole world.

The Greek *paraklētos* literally means "one who is called to your side in your time of need" and is translated in English as "comforter," "counselor," "helper," and "advocate." I have always wondered why no translator has used or coined the word "empowerer," since Jesus is the One who baptizes in the Holy Spirit. It is important to note that there is a twofold intercession going on in and on behalf of believers. Intercession is communicated through the Holy Spirit who Himself prays from within us with groans that cannot be uttered, communicating in the Spirit what we are unable to understand or even put into words. Then there is Jesus, our great High Priest, who is at the same time interceding in the Holy of Holies of heaven on our behalf.

Dr. Mary Healy, a friend of mine who is one of the leading biblical scholars in the Catholic Church, is also the general editor of a commentary on the New Testament and has written commentaries on Mark and Hebrews. She is also the primary person representing the biblical foundation for the charismatic renewal within Roman Catholicism. I so appreciate Dr. Healy's insights regarding the understanding of Jesus in Hebrews that I want to draw from her commentary to give us greater insight into the similarities and differences between the Old Testament high priest under the Law and Jesus, our great High Priest. Dr. Healy wrote:

Only in light of the Old Testament background is it possible to appreciate the transformation in the priesthood that takes place in Christ (see [Hebrews] 7:12). When an ordinary man was made a priest, he required *separation* from others in order to relate to God. But when the Son of God through whom the universe was created (1:2) becomes a priest, it is his *solidarity* with human beings that must be assured. Thus Hebrews does not say that in order for Christ to become a high priest he had to be separated from others; rather, "he had to be made like his brethren in every respect, so that he might become a merciful and faithful high priest" (2:17 RSV).

Hebrews 5 begins to explain this transformation of priesthood. As with every aspect of Christian faith, the relation between the old covenant and the new involves both continuity and discontinuity. On the one hand, Christ is the perfect realization of all that priesthood stood for in the Old Testament; on the other hand, he realizes it in an unexpected way, not fully conforming to the old pattern but elevating it to a new level.[4]

JESUS IS OUR GREAT HIGH PRIEST FOREVER

Jesus is without beginning of days or end of life. He is eternal and forever, our great High Priest. As Hebrews 7:3 describes Him, "Without father, without mother, without genealogy, having neither beginning of days nor end of life, but resembling the Son of God, he remains a priest forever" (NRSV).

Jesus is our righteousness, our justification, our sanctification, our intercessor, and our great sympathetic High Priest. He is the only way to the Father. He draws us to the Father by the Holy Spirit who enables us to believe the gospel, having convinced us of our sin, of righteousness, and of a judgment to come. The Holy Spirit also convicts us of the truth of the gospel and awakens us to be aware of how lost we are and of our great need of Jesus.

It is the Holy Spirit who enabled me to respond to the gospel of Jesus. I thank almighty God, Three in One, for the work of salvation—past, present, and future. All praise to God the Father, God the Son, and God the Holy Spirit!

In answer to Pilate's question of why Jesus had to die, Scripture says that Jesus died to become our great High Priest.

JESUS DIED SO THAT WE MIGHT BE FORGIVEN

Yom Kippur, or the Day of Atonement, is considered the holiest day of the year in Judaism. For approximately twenty-five hours, Jews observe Yom Kippur with fasting and prayer centered around the themes of repentance and atonement. In Hebrew, *Yom* means "day." *Kippur* is derived from the Hebrew for "to atone," and also means "to cleanse" and "to ransom" (*kofer*). The book of Leviticus, in chapter 16, establishes Yom Kippur while also teaching about forgiveness.

To understand the Day of Atonement and its fulfillment in Jesus' death, one needs to read both Leviticus and the book of Hebrews. In so doing, we find out that Jesus is the typological fulfillment of the high priest of Leviticus, who intercedes for our sins so that we might be forgiven. In Old Testament days, on the Day of Atonement, two goats were brought forth. The high priest would slit the throat of the first goat, then take its blood and put it on his right thumb, his right ear lobe, and his vestment. Only after he had shed the blood of the first goat and put it on himself was he given the right to enter into the Holy of Holies, to the mercy seat, where God would come down.

There, at the mercy seat, the high priest would intercede for his people—for their sins—and they would be forgiven. Once this was accomplished, the high priest would come out and lay his hands on the head of the second goat. Then the second goat would be taken outside the camp, symbolically bearing away the sins of the people.

When we look at Jesus, we see that He fulfilled all these types. The angel who came to Mary didn't tell her to name Him Jesus because He would save the people *in* their sins. Instead the angel said He will save people *from* their sins. If we focus only on the first goat whose blood was shed, rather than also on the second goat who was set free, we are not recognizing the fullness of the gospel.

The hypergrace message overemphasizes justification or imputed righteousness without balancing it with sanctification (the second goat of Leviticus 16) with its emphasis upon grace as empowerment to have victory over sin rather than sin having victory over us. In its extreme forms there is no place for the Christian to confess their sin, and even to do so would be seen as not believing in their justification. Often this results in a very worldly and defeated Christian life. The emphasis is grace as undeserved mercy and forgiveness for all sins—past, present, and future—with no emphasis on grace for deliverance from sinful practices.

There is a tendency in this way of thinking to focus only on justification or forgiveness and to ignore sanctification. This is one of the weaknesses of the hypergrace message. While it is strong in its understanding of justification, it lacks a focus on God's way of accomplishing this. Justification is serious business. The sacrifice of Jesus was no trifling matter. The Old Testament people of God understood this.

Because it was such a serious thing to go into God's presence, only the high priest went, and he went with a rope tied around his ankle and bells sewn on the bottom of his gown. As long as the bells could be heard, those outside the Holy of Holies knew the high priest was still moving. If they no longer heard the bells, they assumed he had likely been struck dead in the presence of God and would pull him out from the Holy of Holies by the rope around his ankle because no one else dared go in. If the high priest went into the Holy of Holies to meet God presumptuously rather than by God's way, he would die. Thus, the holiness of God, not just the mercy of God, was emphasized. If the high priest ignored the holiness of God and focused only on His mercy and tried to obtain forgiveness in any other way than how God had clearly laid out, he would die.

IMPUTED RIGHTEOUSNESS

Likewise, it is only through God's way that we can experience what is called imputed righteousness. This is why we can boldly approach the throne of grace in our time of need. We have a great High Priest, Jesus, who has been tempted without sin. We can boldly approach because the blood of Jesus has been applied to us, for our justification. We don't need bells and a rope.

Yet, imputed righteousness and forgiveness is not enough. John Wesley understood this. If sin hurts us, we are not only forgiven for the sins of our past; we also need to receive power to break the sin pattern because sin is not just a rule.

Sin is an understanding of God regarding what hurts us, of our fallen nature that needs to be redeemed. So, it is the second goat that represents sanctification. Not only does God declare you "right" and say you are righteous, but now what God has imputed to you, He wants to work in you. God has given you the right to come into His presence through Jesus. Now He wants the Holy Spirit to be at work in you to set you free and create a new nature so that His laws are not just written on tablets of stone, but on your heart.

HOLY SPIRIT CONVICTION: JUSTIFICATION AND SANCTIFICATION

When my wife, DeAnne, and I started a church in St. Louis, there was a man in our congregation named D.J. I would travel to St. Louis and stay with D.J. one night a week for a few weeks in order to scout out locations for our church plant. D.J. lived in an apartment complex known for partying. He had been married three or four times and was a mess when I met him. Then, I led him to the Lord and D.J. got saved. After that, we used the party place to evangelize. We would do baptisms in the hot tub, right in front of everyone, especially in the wintertime.

Right after he was saved, D.J. had sex with someone and felt terrible afterward. He felt guilty and said it wasn't fun to sin anymore. You see, D.J. needed the Holy Spirit to bring him into who he was in Christ. The fact that he felt terrible after engaging in sin was an indication that he had truly been born again, marked for Jesus. His behavior was grieving the Spirit of God in him. This kind of Holy Spirit conviction is true change. It is justification *and* sanctification. D.J. eventually helped to bring many people to the Lord.

I grew up Baptist, and Baptists were teetotalers, meaning they didn't believe you should drink any alcohol. Once, D.J. and I were getting ready to have ten to fifteen unsaved people come to his apartment to talk with them about God. D.J. had a bar, and he thought we should offer the unsaved people a drink when they came in because "that's how good hosts behaved," as he thought. I didn't want people to drink because I wanted to make sure it was God touching them and not the whiskey. I wanted them to know it was the Lord who caused them to feel the conviction, not the alcohol. I wanted them to get drunk on supernatural wine, new wine—the Holy Spirit—not natural wine. It was then that I realized that my teetotalism was more cultural than biblical.

Our experience, not just our belief system, is so very important. God says, "I make you righteous before Me." However, God wants to make us not only righteous before Him—a judicial righteousness—He also wants to make us truly free, having the power to live rightly before Him. There's a saying that the boat is to be in the water, but the water is not to be in the boat. In other words, we are to be in the world, but not of the world.

God's legalism is not a superficial legalism. It is a passion in our hearts for the kingdom, for the rule of God. Jesus was the most holy person to ever walk the face of the earth, but He wasn't very religious. There is a holiness that believers can fall into that can alienate sinners, making them feel uncomfortable around us, but that is not the kind of holiness Jesus walked in.

THE FORGIVENESS OF GOD

When I was a Baptist pastor in seminary, DeAnne and I would drive up to our weekend pastorate, one hundred miles from our mobile home. We were living on $120 a week. By the time I had finished my last class on Friday and come home, DeAnne would have already packed the car, and we would spend our last dollars filling up the gas tank. Living that way was exciting then. We knew what it was like to be poor, but there was joy in us.

As a student pastor, I would preach in various places. I remember the day I was preaching in a church in Indiana, and a woman I'll call Lou (not her real name) jumped up and ran out the door so fast that when she hit the door, it flew back and hit the brick wall. Now, Lou was a big woman—about six feet tall and heavyset—and had a reputation for being a dangerous person. I had been warned that she prided herself on being able to beat men up.

Lou didn't know me and had never heard me preach before. When I said, "I remember when I was a little boy, my dad told me he wanted to live his life so that he could look back and want his three children to walk in his footsteps. His words touched my heart even as a small boy," it triggered something in Lou. I knew I had to go visit her.

Lou lived in a trailer park that was about as rough as she was. Not sure how she would respond, I was relieved when she invited me in. As we talked, she got out a thick scrapbook full of newspaper clippings about herself. Every article was about some awful behavior of hers—public drunkenness, disorderly conduct, battery, assault. Lou told me that she used to be proud of her behavior, so proud in fact that she made that scrapbook. But now she wasn't proud anymore because she was pregnant with a little girl and didn't want her daughter to walk in her footsteps. "I need to be changed," she said. "I need to be saved. I need real conversion."

Lou didn't understand how to become a Christian. She didn't know anything about God, but she knew she needed to be changed. I knew God was dealing with her, and I tried to get her to pray with me to ask God to forgive her, and to surrender her life to Jesus. I knew she needed salvation, but she didn't understand what conversion meant or what salvation meant. She just wanted something real.

I decided to give her some books to read about people like herself who had been saved—people who had been drug dealers and gang members. I wanted her to read *Run Baby Run*,[1] about Nicky Cruz, and *The Cross and the Switchblade*,[2] about David Wilkerson and Teen Challenge. Lou took those books and started reading and coming to church regularly, and I continued talking with her, trying to help her understand the gospel and her need to accept Jesus.

Then one day Lou told me she was facing more prison time. This time, though, she would not be going to the county jail, but to the state penitentiary, for stabbing a man with a butcher knife at a bachelor party. Lou's whole family were alcoholics, including her parents and siblings. There was a lot of captivity in her family, a lot of bondage. She was drunk when she went to the bachelor party. When a fight broke out, afraid her younger brother was going to be beaten to death, she stabbed his assailant.

Lou needed salvation and she knew it. Long story short, I saw her trying to make changes, so I wrote a letter to the judge and went to court the day she was sentenced. When the judge asked me to step up to his desk, he looked at me and said, "Based upon your letter, I'm led to let her go." He was so moved by what I had written about Lou and the changes she was making that he gave her sixty days, at which time she would be released to me. I was told that he could have sentenced her to as much as sixty years.

Every weekend after that, DeAnne and I would drive an additional one hundred miles to Indianapolis to visit Lou in prison. At each visit, I would try to lead her to the Lord, but she would never pray the prayer of surrender and faith, asking for forgiveness. She just wanted her salvation, conversion, and regeneration to be real. Then one Sunday, as soon as Lou came through the door, I knew she'd been born again by the look on her face and the joy that was there. When she sat down, I said, "You got saved, didn't you?" She said she had. Then I asked her how she knew it was real.

"There was a prayer in one of those books you gave me," she replied. "I just kept reading it over and over and decided to go for it. I prayed that prayer and started crying and felt so good. I knew it was real because I was so happy. My guilt has left me. I'm praying that the man I stabbed and his family would also come to know Jesus."

There is a difference between forgiveness of sin and facing consequences. Lou's words revealed that she had come face-to-face with the reality of the consequences of sin.

THE GIFT OF FAITH

There Lou was, a single mom, a felon with a rap. And on top of that Lou knew she was "nothing to look at," as she put it. At that point in her life she had no faith of finding a husband to share her life with, but I did. I had a gift of faith.

"Lou," I said one day, "I don't know how, but I honestly believe that if you keep Jesus first in your life, He will bring your mate to you. He will put your life back together."

Soon after that, Lou was released from prison. Her first Sunday home, we went to the river behind the church and I baptized her. Every one of her brothers and her parents watched her baptism. And, as time went on, everyone saw the miraculous transformation that occurred in her life. God began to use her as an ambassador for Christ. Before that year was over, I baptized most of her family. They were all delivered from the power of their guilt and addictions. Two of them became deacons in the church, and Lou became a Sunday school teacher. For the next eighteen years, I received a picture at Christmas of Lou's little girl becoming a young woman. Truly the mercy of God was present in Lou's life.

THE MERCY OF GOD MADE
AVAILABLE TO US IN JESUS

If you want to see the mercy of God made available to us, read the Gospels. There, particularly in the gospel of Luke, but also in John's gospel, you will encounter Jesus, who has love for the unlovely, grace for the sinner, and concern for the marginalized. Luke 19 records the story of one of the most despised, marginalized persons of first-century Israel—the tax collector. Matthew 18:17 reveals how tax collectors were seen in such a negative light: "If they still refuse to listen, tell it to the church; and if they refuse to listen even to the church, treat them as you would a pagan or a tax collector."

A similar modern-day situation was seen in France after the Second World War. Those who worked for and socialized with the Nazis while they occupied France were despised and shamed. The women had their hair cut off publicly. Like the first-century tax collectors, those who betrayed their fellow man to the Nazis were despised.

Yet, in Luke 19 Jesus went to the home of a tax collector named Zacchaeus, a *chief* tax collector who had become wealthy by cheating the people, and He forgave Zacchaeus.

My friend Bob Ekblad is an Old Testament professor with a heart for the marginalized. He has worked with the poorest of people in Nicaragua, established a community in Washington State to help the poor, and gone to some of the worst prisons on earth to hold Bible studies. One of the many books he has written is called *Reading the Bible with the Damned*. While he was teaching at our Global School of Supernatural Ministry, he shared a powerful story.

Bob had gone to a prison in Latin America to conduct a Bible study with the prisoners. The night before, he had a dream of a certain man with a distinguishing tattoo. When he went to the prison the next day, he asked if he could speak with the most notorious prisoner. When he met this prisoner, Bob noticed that the man had the tattoo he had seen in his dream. God had also revealed to Bob some very personal things about this prisoner that no one knew but the prisoner himself. During their meeting, Bob shared the information he had prophetically received in the dream.

The prisoner's hardness of heart was broken by the supernatural display of God's love for him and the information Bob had received. Weeping, he asked Jesus to forgive him as he committed his life to Christ.

After Bob left the prison, he found out that just a few days later that prisoner had been transferred to another prison where many members of an opposing gang were incarcerated. They captured this new convert to Jesus, who had been the leader of a rival gang, cut off his head, and played soccer with it. The mercy of God for this man came through Bob's dream and subsequent visit, extending eternal life supernaturally to this prisoner just a few days before he was murdered. God loves the marginalized. His grace reaches into the darkest places.

GOD LOVES THE SINNER

John's gospel tells of another marginalized person. In John 4:4–42 we find the story of the woman at the well. Jesus, a Jew, stopped at a Samaritan village where He met a Samaritan woman whom He asked for water. Jews despised the Samaritans, thinking of them as half-breeds, to the point that a Jew would go out of the way to avoid going through the region of Samaria. Furthermore, in the culture at that time, men did not speak with women in public except for those in their own families.

Scripture tells that Jesus supernaturally knew things about this woman—that she had a tragic record with men. She had been married five times, and the man she "now has" was not her husband. Yet, in spite of all her shame and failure, though she had truly been marginalized, Jesus offered her eternal life. The woman was shocked that Jesus, a Jew, spoke to her, and was amazed by His revelations about her life.

We don't know whether she was impressed or rattled by her

conversation with Jesus and His gracious offer, but for whatever reason, she left her water pot and returned to her village to tell everyone, "Come, see a man who told me everything I ever did. Could this be the Messiah?" (John 4:29). Because of her testimony, many believed in Jesus. In fact, many went out to see Him and invited Him to stay in their village, which He did for two days, as He shared with them. As a result of His words, many more became believers.

Another powerful story in the Bible of Jesus and the marginalized is that of the sinful woman in the Pharisee's home. This story is recorded in Luke 7:36–50. First of all, I find it interesting that Jesus was willing to even go to the Pharisee's home. Some of His most critical rebukes were in regard to and directed at Pharisees. Also, how this particular woman was able to come into the Pharisee's home is interesting to me. I will have to ask her about it when I meet her in heaven. Tradition has associated her sin with being a prostitute, although the text doesn't say what her sin was.

Anyway, however she did it, she crashed the dinner and came into the Pharisee's home with an alabaster jar of perfume. Verse 38 tells us that, as she stood behind Jesus, she was weeping. It says that she wet His feet with her tears then dried them with her hair, kissed His feet, and anointed them with the expensive perfume. The fact that this was expensive perfume may indicate that if she was a prostitute, she must have been what today would be an expensive and attractive call girl with well-to-do clients. But perhaps her sin involved something else. We don't really know.

When Simon the Pharisee saw what was happening, he concluded that Jesus couldn't be a legitimate prophet, for if He were, He would have known what kind of woman was touching Him—that she was a sinner. A Pharisee, a separated one, would cross the street so as not to be contaminated by unclean people. The Pharisees couldn't understand how Jesus could be holy and allow an unclean sinful person to touch Him. The story ends with the following dialogue between Jesus, Simon the Pharisee, and the unnamed sinful woman:

Jesus answered him, "Simon, I have something to tell you."

"Tell me, teacher," he said.

"Two people owed money to a certain moneylender. One owed him five hundred denarii, and the other fifty. Neither of them had the money to pay him back, so he forgave the debts of both. Now which of them will love him more?"

Simon replied, "I suppose the one who had the bigger debt forgiven."

"You have judged correctly," Jesus said.

Then he turned toward the woman and said to Simon, "Do you see this woman? I came into your house. You did not give me any water for my feet, but she wet my feet with her tears and wiped them with her hair. You did not give me a kiss, but this woman, from the time I entered, has not stopped kissing my feet. You did not put oil on my head, but she has poured perfume on my feet. Therefore, I tell you, her many sins have been forgiven—as her great love has shown. But whoever has been forgiven little loves little."

Then Jesus said to her, "Your sins are forgiven."

The other guests began to say among themselves, "Who is this who even forgives sins?"

Jesus said to the woman, "Your faith has saved you; go in peace." (vv. 40–50)

THE MERCY OF GOD IN MOZAMBIQUE

When I read this story from Luke, I can't help but reflect upon two incidents that I personally experienced that demonstrate the great mercy of God.

One occurred on the first of several visits I made to Mozambique to work with Heidi and Rolland Baker. One day, Heidi took me to the city dump, a place where she regularly ministers to the people who live there. Later that day, we went to an abandoned area of the city that had been impacted by the civil war. People there were living in tents and in parts of abandoned buildings. Together we stepped into one such abandoned room where an older woman was living. She was a former prostitute whom Heidi had led to Jesus.

The room was rather dark with no windows, lit by a few candles. As I looked around the room I saw several faces of young women, or more accurately older girls, who had become prostitutes. I watched their faces as Heidi spoke to them in their native dialect. She was telling them about Jesus. As she did, tears began to flow down their cheeks as the Holy Spirit drew these poor, marginalized girls to the Father. Nearly all of them gave their lives to Jesus that night.

The following Sunday, during worship, I noticed several young worshipers dressed in white who were dancing and singing unto God—Father, Son, and Holy Spirit. Heidi came up to me and told me that almost all the older girls in the worship group had been prostitutes or prostituted by their families before coming to Jesus. Now they were experiencing new life. Jesus still seeks not the righteous but sinners, welcoming them with His love and forgiveness.

So, in answer to Pilate's question, "Why did Jesus have to die?" Jesus died so God's power of grace and forgiveness could be made available to us. He had to die so that people like you and I could be set free and become a new creation; so that we could be forgiven and God could be just and righteous. This aspect of forgiveness pertains to His role as the great High Priest, and at the same time the sacrificial Lamb of God. God's way of imputed righteousness is opened to us through Jesus. His way is also to impart power to us to live righteously, to become what He declares us to be. Imputed and imparted righteousness.

ten

JESUS DIED SO THAT WE MAY HAVE ETERNAL LIFE

*He died for us so that, whether we are awake or asleep, we may
live together with him.*

—1 THESSALONIANS 5:10

The great promise of eternal life in Christ for believers stands in stark contrast to the darkness of death and all that such a darkness holds for those outside of Christ. Yet, what does it mean for believers, either awake or asleep, to "live together with Him"? In simplest terms, it means that Christ's death on the cross opened heaven to us for all eternity. When our physical bodies die on this earth, our souls will "sleep" with Jesus until His glorious return, at which time we will be together with Him fully in both body and soul. The living soul is both spirit and body. The death of the body is portrayed as sleep, a way of speaking of death. Though the body is asleep, the spirit of the person is alive and is with the Lord, and when He comes, our spirit will be clothed with a glorious resurrection body that is incorruptible.

Without the cross, our earthly bodies would be forever shut up in the grave—we would not experience a resurrection of our physical body. But thanks be to God for the resurrection of Jesus who leads us in His triumph up out of the grave to live together with Him in body and soul for all eternity in the beautiful peace of His presence! This death from which we are saved is both a physical death and a spiritual one. Dead in our sins, we are now able to come alive in Christ, sanctified and justified by His blood, to live a life of sweet communion with Him forever.

Eternal life is more than everlasting life. There is a quality of heaven to eternal life that is greatly to be desired. Think of it—everlasting life could be a very bad thing if the quality of that life was not good.

Years ago, I heard an illustration about the difference between everlasting and eternal life. There were two young men who were going through Appalachia selling Bibles and religious books. They came upon a dirt lane that went up to an old dilapidated house. Outside in the backyard was a young mother with five children running around playing. The mother was doing the laundry on a washboard in a galvanized tub and hanging the washed laundry on the clothesline that ran between two trees.

The young men were not only selling Bibles, they were also sharing their faith in an effort to evangelize to the people they met. As they were sharing the gospel, which they called *good news*, with this young mom, when they got to the part about everlasting life, she turned her head to look the young men in the eyes and said, "Look around. What makes you think that the prospect of living forever is good news to me? My life, as it is, would not be a good thing to endure forever."

These young evangelists hadn't explained the difference between the kind of eternal life available to us in the cross of Christ versus just living forever. It's about quality, not endless duration. Jesus died so that we can have eternal life, which begins when we are born of the Spirit and never ends. However, it is a glorious type of life with Jesus that is beyond description.

GOD'S GLORIOUS ETERNAL LIFE FOR BELIEVERS

Eternal life is more than everlasting; it is life on a higher plane, life of a higher quality, a richer, fuller life. My mother experienced this kind of life while she was still in her early twenties. I was about six, my brother was four and a half, and my sister three and a half when this happened. We were at a home for a time of prayer and worship with some people from the church. At one point my mother headed outside to warm up the car before taking us little children out. As she walked toward the car, suddenly she was caught in the power of the Spirit, causing her to fall to the ground. As she was later able to tell us, her spirit left her body and went through dimensions of turbulence followed by peace. This happened several times, after which she found herself in the most beautiful place she had ever seen. The feelings she had of love and being loved, of joy, of perfect peace, were beyond her ability to put into words.

Then a man came to her. Although He didn't look like the pictures she had seen of Jesus, she knew it was Him. He sat down beside her and they communicated, without words, spirit to spirit. As she shared her struggles, He told her that the struggles she was experiencing would eventually come to an end and that she would be fine—that everything would be okay. Then He smiled and touched her knee with His hand. Suddenly she felt her spirit going back toward her body as cycles of turbulence followed by peace occurred until finally she was back fully in her body.

My mother was so affected by this experience that it worried my father. She would walk through the house muttering, "It is so beautiful, it is so peaceful, it is so wonderful. I don't want to stay here. I want to go back." The fact that she had three small children and a husband seemed to have been lost to her. She was consumed with a passion to get back to that place of peace with Jesus, where she had experienced the quality of eternal life available to those who are in Christ. She was forever changed.

For the next fifty years, my mother was unable to share this experience without weeping, as she struggled for words to explain the utter sweetness of what had happened to her. Then, on Christmas Eve 2018, my mother again left her body, this time just two months shy of eighty-five, and went home to spend all eternity in that beautiful, peaceful place of total love and acceptance with Jesus, where she is once again experiencing eternal life in the power of the cross. I know that one day she will receive a glorified body with the dimensional aspects of both a spiritual body and a corporeal body.

A number of years after my mother's experience, when I was in college, I had the opportunity to interview the two men from the church who had found my mother laying on the ground that night. They explained that she had no pulse, no breath, and her body had grown cold and clammy. Based upon their observations, I believe that my mother died, or at least that her spirit left her body, which I believe occurs at death. Her experience shaped my perspective on life after death for those who are in Christ. Whenever I conduct a funeral for believers, I share my mother's story as a way to comfort those who are grieving.

LOOK UPON JESUS AND LIVE

In the book of Numbers, we find a significant historical event in the history of the Jewish people that gives us insight into the death and resurrection of Jesus, and what it makes available to believers. In Numbers 21:4–9 we find the people of God traveling from Mount Hor along the route to the Red Sea, to go around Edom. Scripture says that they grew impatient upon the way and spoke against God and Moses saying, "Why have you brought us up out of Egypt to die in the wilderness? There is no bread! There is no water! And we detest this miserable food!" (v. 5).

In response, God sent venomous snakes among them that bit the people, causing many to die (v. 6). Then, the people came to Moses and, acknowledging their sin, they asked Moses to pray that the Lord would take away the snakes, so Moses prayed (v. 7).

Do you see the parallel? Dead in their sin, they cried out to God for help. And help He did! Scripture says that the Lord instructed Moses to make a snake, put it on a pole, and anyone who has been bitten could look upon the snake on the pole and live (vv. 8–9). Fast-forward to Jesus in John 3.

> And as Moses lifted up the bronze snake on a pole in the wilderness, so the Son of Man must be lifted up, so that everyone who believes in him will have eternal life. For this is how God loved the world: He gave his one and only Son, so that everyone who believes in him will not perish but have eternal life. God sent his Son into the world not to judge the world, but to save the world through him. (vv. 14–17 NLT)

Jesus was lifted up in the crucifixion, lifted up in the resurrection, and lifted up in the ascension. However, the universality of verse 17 must be interpreted through the particularity of verses 15 and 16. Verse 17 doesn't mean that everyone will be saved (and enjoy eternal life). Salvation is limited to those who believe in Jesus. Author Michael McClymond pointed out that Jesus did not say, "For God so loved the world that none should perish but all should have eternal life."[1] That is the message of universalism, which leaves Jesus out of the equation. The Bible is clear here that there are two distinct outcomes regarding life after death—one with Jesus for all eternity, and one separated from Jesus for all eternity.

In answer to Pilate's question of why Jesus had to die, Scripture says that Jesus died so that we might have eternal life.

It is in our glorified bodies that we will enjoy a renewed heaven and earth, where neither pain nor sorrow nor aging nor lack will ever be felt again. This is why the apostle Paul told believers not to mourn or grieve as the world mourns or grieves, because through the cross we have both everlasting life and eternal life.

eleven

JESUS DIED SO THAT WE MIGHT BE BORN AGAIN

He came to Jesus at night and said, "Rabbi, we know that You are a teacher who has come from God. For no one could perform the signs You are doing if God were not with him." Jesus replied, "Truly, truly, I tell you, no one can see the kingdom of God unless he is born again." "How can a man be born when he is old?" Nicodemus asked. "Can he enter his mother's womb a second time to be born?" Jesus answered, "Truly, truly, I tell you, no one can enter the kingdom of God unless he is born of water and the Spirit. Flesh is born of flesh, but spirit is born of the Spirit."

—JOHN 3:2–6 BSB

To understand what Jesus meant when He told Nicodemus of the necessity of being born again in order to "see" the kingdom of God, one must realize that He was speaking of the contrast between nature and grace rather than of a philos relationship. Philos is an earthly love like that which exists among family members and friends. It is a human type of affection. Jesus wanted Nicodemus to understand that there is a spiritual vision needed if one is to see the kingdom of God and understand God's love, and that spiritual vision comes only when one is spiritually born anew of the Spirit of God. This new birth brings with it a change of heart that moves a person from hostility and indifference toward God to a place of loving Him and longing to live for Him and with Him.

The prophet Ezekiel spoke of this new birth hundreds of years before Jesus walked the earth, as he spoke the words of God to the people of Israel, who had profaned his holy name among the nations: "And I will give you a new heart, and a new spirit I will put within you. And I will remove the heart of stone from your flesh and give you a heart of flesh" (Ezek. 36:26 ESV).

To be born again is more than a doctrine for me. It is my family's experience. My mother grew up as a child of alcoholics, hiding behind doors as alcoholism played itself out in her family, afraid of her dad and uncle when they were drunk. My mother's father, my grandfather, was once a bad man. I thank God that I have no memories of him as a raging drunk who threw furniture. My grandmother was illiterate. They met and she became pregnant while he was married to another woman. He eventually married my grandmother, but continued to womanize.

My father was raised in a non-Christian home and he cussed like a sailor. He was at one time not a good man either. One day both he and my grandfather went to this little Baptist church. I'm not sure why they went, but they did, and it was there that they heard the gospel and came under conviction. With newfound faith that they would be forgiven, they both went to the altar, the mourner's bench, and were born again. From that moment on they were lovers of Jesus, new creations. I got a new dad and a new grandfather who never touched my grandmother in anger again. He never touched another woman in unfaithfulness again. He never touched another drop of alcohol again.

That night my grandfather was delivered from the tormenting demons in his life, their power over him broken. God put him through a one-step program that works better than any other. The power of the gospel is real; deliverance is real. God's redemptive work in us makes us new creations.

SURRENDERING ALL TO JESUS

I grew up in churches that had been deeply influenced by the revival culture of the Second Great Awakening and the "new measures" of Charles Finney. The main theme in that stream of the church was to be born again so that you could go to heaven. To be born again meant that you came under the conviction of the Holy Spirit for your sins. When this happened, you went forward to the front of the church to a small bench. These plain wooden benches were called the mourner's bench or the altar and were descriptive of what they symbolized. Think back to the Old Testament for a minute, to what happened at altars in those days.

An altar was the place where the sacrificial animal was slain for the forgiveness of sin, or as an act of worship with a desire to become closer to God. Do you see the similarity?

The mourner's bench of my childhood was a physical place where you experienced the joy caused by the Holy Spirit coming into your life with the love of God, the joy of salvation, and the assurance that you were forgiven. As you knelt at the bench, you would "pray through" until the sorrow left you and was replaced by the peace, joy, and love of God that would suddenly come upon you. Fear of hell was replaced with assurance of heaven. That was the religious culture I grew up in. It was a culture that said if you didn't know when you were born again, then you hadn't really been born again—saved and converted.

As the young pastor of the First United Church of Christ, I began to encounter Christians who were saved but had no recollection of the moment of their salvation. Although they had no mourner's bench experience, I could see that their salvation was real. This brought me to a point where I realized that the model of salvation I had grown up with was not the only one. I had a dramatic focus on the type of salvation experience the apostle Paul had on the road to Damascus. Others had a Timothy experience of being born and raised in a Christian home, with Christian values and a knowledge of God. Their understanding of being born again was less emotional, gentler, and not focused on the moment of salvation, but on a process of coming to know God. What I had thought was normal was actually not.

When I say there is more than one way to become a new creation, to be born again, I don't mean that there is more than one way to God. I strongly believe salvation is only in and through Jesus. He is the only way to the Father, and salvation is in His name alone. What I am saying is that there is more than one way a person can come to know God, and to understand that they are known by God. In 2 Corinthians, Paul said, "Therefore, if anyone is in Christ, he is a new creation. The old has passed away; behold, the new has come" (5:17 ESV).

The emphasis of the First and Second Great Awakenings was upon being born again. I believe there is much to be said for this tradition, which focused on the momentary experience of salvation. My dear friend Bill Johnson cannot tell me the moment of his salvation. Yet there is no doubt in my mind that Bill has been born again. He is a new creation just as I am, but God brought us to that point in different ways. Our lives and experiences are different. Yet we are both born of the Spirit. Bill is one of my heroes of the faith.

THE STRONG MAN HAS BEEN BOUND

A few years ago God brought a young pastor to Global School named William Wood. William has since become one of my associate ministers. William's born-again experience is quite dramatic and extremely different from mine. William grew up in Alabama. His parents were bound by addiction to alcohol, did not believe in God, and did not take him to church. Though William grew up in the "Bible Belt," as the South is often referred to, not one person ever shared the gospel with him. He had never read the Bible.

By his mid-teens, William was an alcoholic and a drug addict. He took all kinds of drugs and went through two rehabilitation programs, but was helpless to stop his addictions. His relationship with his parents was destroyed by these addictions that brought with them a lifestyle of lying, stealing, cheating—whatever it took to secure more drugs. At age twenty, William woke up in the intensive care unit of the local hospital. The police found him lying in the street unconscious, dying of a meth overdose, his pockets full of paraphernalia and meth.

After five days in intensive care, the doctor came into his room and told William that his kidneys had shut down, and his liver and other organs were shutting down, and unless they could reverse the organ failure, he would die. A lot of people cry out to God on their death bed, but William didn't because he didn't believe in God. He just lay there in bed, upset at the thought of dying so young.

During the night a bright light shone into his room. Out of the light stepped a man in a white robe with brown hair. As he moved from the foot of the bed toward William, William could feel the energy flowing into and through his body. He was also very much aware of feeling a profound, powerful love. Then a spring of water began to come out of the wall near his feet and flowed across the room and out the other wall. The man turned to the stream and began washing his hands in it. At that moment William heard the audible voice of God speak to him.

"William," God said, "these waters will cleanse and purify you when you believe that Jesus is the Christ."

William cried out with all that was in him, "Yes!" as sensations of energy continued to flow through his body.

The next morning the doctor ran about five hours of tests, but he couldn't find any explanation as to why all William's organs were working. And not only were they working, they were like new organs. The doctor said it was as if William had never touched a single drop of alcohol or taken a single drug.

God healed William, delivering him from the powers of sin and the flesh—from the power of demonic beings. He had been born again of God's Spirit and reconciled to God. He had heard the gospel for the first time from God Himself. William was reconciled to God by accepting the gospel that Jesus was the Christ and by receiving forgiveness through what Jesus did at the cross.

On the cross, Jesus bound the strong man—the devil—and ever since He has been entering the strong man's house and setting the captives free. And that's not all Jesus did on the cross. He also removed our sins so that we could be made righteous, justified, forgiven—a new creation. William is certainly a new creation. Today he is a mighty preacher of the gospel. But there is more to his story.

PAID IN FULL

When the police found William lying unconscious in the street with his pockets full of drug paraphernalia, they had to fill out a report and bring charges against him. As this was his third offense, the law demanded a mandatory sentence in the penitentiary. When William entered the courtroom to face the charges, the judge called him to the front. "Mr. Wood," he said, "I am not going to be able to charge you with anything today. Somehow, all the evidence of your offense is missing. Without the evidence we can't charge you. However, I am going to charge you with court costs of $666."

At that moment William's father stood in the courtroom and said, "I will pay it in full, Your Honor." In addition, the hospital forgave *all* the costs for William's treatment for his five days in the hospital.

What William experienced is a great example of what Paul wrote in Colossians 2:13–14: "When you were dead in your sins and in the uncircumcision of your flesh, God made you alive with Christ. He forgave us all our sins, having canceled the charge of our legal indebtedness, which stood against us and condemned us; he has taken it away, nailing it to the cross." With the power of sin destroyed in his life, William experienced a newfound freedom from drugs and alcohol (he never had withdrawals), becoming a new creation with a new spirit and right heart, producing new morals of righteousness. This experience is available to all who believe on the name of Jesus Christ. By His Spirit, God enlightens all who are made spiritually aware to salvation: "But to all who did receive Him, to those who believed in His name, He gave the right to become children of God— children born not of blood, nor of the desire or will of man, but born of God" (John 1:12–13 BSB).

In answer to Pilate's question of why Jesus had to die, Scripture says that Jesus died so that we might be born again.

twelve

JESUS DIED TO DISPLAY THE JUSTICE AND HOLINESS OF THE TRIUNE GOD

The Lord is not slow in keeping his promise, as some understand slowness. Instead he is patient with you, not wanting anyone to perish, but everyone to come to repentance.

—2 PETER 3:9

Since the foundation of the world, God has been on a mission to reconcile two unchangeable, yet seemingly contradictory, attributes of His nature. On the one hand, God is perfectly holy. There is no sin allowed in His presence. Yet on the other hand, God is perfectly loving. He loves us so much that He would give *anything* to have us in His presence (John 3:16). God doesn't want "any to perish but for all to come to repentance" (2 Peter 3:9 NASB). Yet at the same time, the wages of our sin "is death" (Rom. 6:23).

So here we are, inexorably sinful, born into sin; and when left to our own devices, we continue to sin. Our hearts are "deceitful . . . and desperately wicked" (Jer. 17:9 NKJV). Yet God loves us and wants to be with us. But He simply cannot let our sin go unpunished. Such an oversight would be a violation of His law, a compromise of His perfect justice and absolute holiness.

What all this means is that apart from some divine rescue plan, we are shut out from heaven. Because how can God punish our sin and still love us at the same time? How can He be perfectly holy and true to His Word, yet fully loving and accepting of us at the same time with all our faults, sins, and failures? The answer is found in His blood covenant made on the cross.

THERE HAS TO BE BLOOD— THE BLOOD OF JESUS

Blood covenants are a common theme across ancient cultures. In fact, one constant theme throughout every major civilization in human history is that, in order for God to be satisfied, there has to be blood. E. W. Kenyon, a Baptist pastor and founder of Bethel Bible Institute, notes that "there isn't a primitive people in the world, as far as we know, that has not practiced the blood covenant in some form; showing that it had a God given origin and so man has practiced the covenant through all the ages."[1]

In ancient cultures it would be unthinkable to break a bond established by blood. In fact, if someone broke a blood covenant, that person's family members would seek his death in order to avoid the curses that would accompany the violation. As Christians, our legacy is no different. Christianity has its own blood covenant. It began with Abram (Abraham).

The LORD had said to Abram, "Go from your country, your people and your father's household to the land I will show you.

> "I will make you into a great nation,
>> and I will bless you;
> I will make your name great,
>> and you will be a blessing.
> I will bless those who bless you,
>> and whoever curses you I will curse;
> and all peoples on earth
>> will be blessed through you." (Gen. 12:1–3)

Abraham believed in God's promises, and God "accounted it to him for righteousness" (Gen. 15:6 NKJV). Yet even as Abraham reached the final stages of his life, he hadn't *seen* what God had promised. He still had the promise but had yet to see the fulfillment. The culmination of his frustration can be seen in Genesis 15: "But Abram said, 'Lord GOD, what will You give me, seeing I go childless, and the heir of my house is Eliezer of Damascus?' Then Abram said, 'Look, You have given me no offspring; indeed one born in my house is my heir!'" (vv. 2–3 NKJV).

In order to see God's promise, Abraham needed a tangible guarantee from God. He needed something that would allow him to believe that God was going to do what He had said. So God gave him something that no one had ever received before. God gave Abraham a blood covenant.

And he [Abraham] said, "Lord GOD, how shall I know that I will inherit it?"

So He [God] said to him, "Bring Me a three-year-old heifer, a three-year-old female goat, a three-year-old ram, a turtledove, and a young pigeon." Then he brought all these to Him and cut them in two, down the middle, and placed each piece opposite the other; but he did not cut the birds in two. (vv. 8–10 NKJV)

Remember that in ancient culture the blood covenant was the most binding form of agreement that could be established between two people. In the context of Abraham's time and culture, God gave him a guarantee he could understand by telling him to prepare a blood covenant in a specific way. The seemingly odd directive from God, when understood within the cultural context of Abraham's time, would forever change his life—and ours by extension.

Abraham was directed to sacrifice specific animals and spill their blood, then divide them in two and pass through the pieces once to demonstrate his willingness to uphold the agreement. God would then do the same. The expectation was that if either party to the agreement failed to hold up his end of the bargain, he would be cut in two—divided, just like those animals. Of course God would never allow Himself to be divided and Abraham understood this, which is why this was such a powerful agreement for him.

God had a role to play in this as well. He had promised Abraham a son and to make him (Abraham) a great nation. This blood covenant was God's guarantee of His promises to Abraham. The story of this blood covenant doesn't end there though. There is more, and this *more* is a stunning revelation of God's great mercy and love.

When it came time for Abraham to pass through the pieces, something strange happened: "Now when the sun was going down, a deep sleep fell upon Abram; and behold, horror and great darkness fell upon him" (v. 12 NKJV). Here was Abraham's chance to enter into a binding agreement with God. Yet, when it was his turn to sign the document, he *fell asleep.* More accurately, God caused Abraham to fall asleep because He had a plan.

And it came to pass, when the sun went down and it was dark, that
behold, there appeared a smoking oven and a burning torch that passed
between those pieces. On the same day the LORD made a covenant with
Abram, saying:

"To your descendants I have given this land, from the river of Egypt
to the great river, the River Euphrates." (vv. 17–18 NKJV)

God knew that Abraham would be completely incapable of holding
up his end of the deal, so He put Abraham to sleep and did something
absolutely astounding. God walked through the pieces on Abraham's behalf.
God passed through the pieces *twice*: once as a "smoking oven," and again
as a "burning torch." The smoking oven represents the pillar of cloud that
led the way for the Israelites in the desert during the day, and the burning torch represents the pillar of fire that gave them light at night. These
manifestations of God's glory to the people of Israel were also used in this
blood covenant with Abraham to demonstrate God's great faithfulness in
keeping His promises.

God was saying to Abraham, "You can never do this yourself, *so I will
do it for you*." God agreed to take on the curse when Abraham failed so that
Abraham would never have to. *Nothing* depended on Abraham. *Everything*
depended on God. This is how our Christian blood covenant is different
from every other blood covenant throughout the course of history.

Thousands of years before the cross of Christ, God made Abraham
a promise. When Abraham entered into covenant with God, God would
perform everything He had promised. But when Abraham failed to
deliver—when he lost faith and lost his way—God would step in to take
the fall. God would die so that His people could live.

God knew that Abraham could never have perfect faith, and He knows
you and I can't either. That is why, since antiquity, God promised to fulfill
our requirement for perfect holiness by dying—by becoming a curse—in

our place. God fulfilled that promise to Abraham generations later in the cross of Jesus Christ. Jesus Christ, God in the flesh, died on the cross for us. Jesus passed through death and conquered the grave so that we would never have to. "Christ has redeemed us from the curse of the law, having become a curse for us" (Gal. 3:13 NKJV). God, the Eternal Son, bore the curse for our sins, bore the legal punishment as our sacrifice. In doing so, God the Father was reconciling the world unto Himself.

When you make a decision to believe in Jesus, what you're really saying is, "Lord, thank You for taking on the punishment I deserve for breaking the covenant; and thank You for giving me the reward I could never deserve for perfectly fulfilling the covenant." Jesus took the curse, so that we could receive the prize.

My heart was convicted of this truth at a young age. As you may recall, I was seven years old. No one is ever too young or too old to be touched by the conviction of God.

WHY THE CROSS? WHY PUNISH US AT ALL?

The brutal death of Jesus on the cross has caused many down through the ages to wonder why death was required at all. Why did God have to punish sin in the first place? How is it fair that God has allowed us to be born into a fallen world through no decision of our own? None of us told our parents to bring us into this world, so how is it "just" for God to ask us to struggle through life until we find Jesus when it wasn't our decision to be here in the first place? And how is it "love" that so many people wander through life without ever finding Jesus at all and end up in Gehenna, the Second Death, as a result?

The Scriptures give us the answers. The prophet Isaiah made it clear that God has never tried to hide anything from us.

> Tell and bring forth your case;
>
> Yes, let them take counsel together.
>
> Who has declared this from ancient time?
>
> Who has told it from that time?
>
> Have not I, the LORD?
>
> And there is no other God besides Me,
>
> A just God and a Savior;
>
> There is none besides Me. (Isa. 45:21 NKJV)

In His great love, God has been telling us about Himself from the beginning of time. "For since the creation of the world His invisible attributes are clearly seen, being understood by the things that are made, even His eternal power and Godhead, so that they are without excuse" (Rom. 1:20 NKJV). Everything around us in creation points to the design of the One who is divine wisdom and creativity itself. None of creation is an accident.

By divine design, God the Creator cannot simply open the doors to heaven and let everyone in. That would violate His standard for holiness and corrupt His divine design with sin. When you think about it, would you want to worship a God who didn't demand perfection? Would you want to spend all eternity in a heaven where evil and sin were allowed? If your answer is no, then by your own standard, your sin would separate you from the perfect and holy God you desire.

The truth is, on our own we are incapable of righteousness. "All of us have become like one who is unclean, and all our righteous acts are like filthy rags" (Isa. 64:6). In the desert, God presented His commandments to the Israelites, and they had the pride to actually believe they could do everything He asked (Ex. 19:7–8). The truth is that we deserve the wrath of God as punishment for our sin. Yet, Christ Himself came in our place to break down the wall of separation that stands between our sinful flesh and God's holy nature. The only way to put to death the declaration of war made in the garden between our sinful flesh and God's holy nature was for God Himself to become flesh and to die. The apostle Paul put it this way:

> For He Himself is our peace, who has made both one, and has broken down the middle wall of separation, having abolished in His flesh the enmity, that is, the law of commandments contained in ordinances, so as to create in Himself one new man from the two, thus making peace, and that He might reconcile them both to God in one body through the cross, thereby putting to death the enmity. (Eph. 2:14–16 NKJV)

Jesus chose to die for our sin, opening the door for us to choose to become the "righteousness of God in Him" (2 Cor. 5:21 NKJV). God didn't kill Jesus on the cross. You did, and I did; we did. And we have to take personal responsibility for it. Jesus died in our place, as the penal substitute for *our* actions, for *our* sin. Beware of distancing yourself from the suffering of the cross like Pilate who washed his hands before the multitude, saying, "I am innocent of this man's blood" (Matt. 27:24). To blame the cross on someone else is to rob it of its benefits and its beauty. Instead, accept the blame.

If you think the cross had nothing to do with you, it becomes just a horror story of an abusive father taking his anger out on an innocent son. It is important to accept personal responsibility for the death of Jesus on the cross. Because if you see yourself as separated and distant from the cross, you will never receive the fullness of its benefits and marvel at its beauty.

The cross of Jesus Christ is for you, for all of us, and because of us, it is a beautiful picture of God Himself—Jesus Christ—offering up His life and accepting the death we deserve. The beauty of the cross is that we don't stop at the place of mourning because Jesus died in our place. We can move beyond mourning to celebrate that Jesus is now alive again, and when we believe, we are alive in Him!

Many years ago when I was still in my twenties, I went to a prison to talk with a man convicted of murder. I shared the gospel with him. He responded, "I can't believe this gospel. It is too easy to be forgiven. There would be no justice if God forgave me so easily that all I had to do was to confess my sins and commit my life to follow Jesus." To which I responded, "It is not too easy. Your forgiveness is free to you, but costly to God. Jesus took your sins and died so you could be forgiven and the power of sin in your life defeated. He died so that you could not just be put right, but also made right. By the power of His Holy Spirit He would give you the power to not only be reckoned righteous, pardoned, but made righteous through the Holy Spirit living inside of you, empowering you to live a holy life, no longer captive to sin's dominion." When this man saw the righteousness of God in Christ and the justice of God exhibited at the cross as I read Colossians 2:13–15 to him, tears filled his eyes. He then surrendered himself to Christ and asked for God's forgiveness.

In answer to Pilate's question of why Jesus had to die, Scripture says that Jesus died to enact the justice and holiness of God. The justice and holiness of God kissed on the cross, perfectly reconciling the two attributes of God's nature. "Mercy and truth have met together; righteousness and peace have kissed" (Ps. 85:10 NKJV). And what an astounding kiss it was! God's righteous anger fell on His only Son, Jesus Christ, so that His perfect peace could fall on us. As believers, our New Testament reality is one of redemption and restoration, as we are lifted up to be seated in heavenly places for all eternity.

thirteen

JESUS DIED TO DEMONSTRATE THE RIGHTEOUSNESS OF GOD

For He made Him who knew no sin to be sin for us, that we might become the righteousness of God in Him.

—2 CORINTHIANS 5:21 NKJV

Scripture says that because you have received Jesus, you have become the *righteousness* of God. Yet, what is the righteousness of God? What does righteousness mean in the Bible? What are the writers of Scripture saying about the character of God when they speak of His righteousness?

THE DIVINE EXCHANGE

Because we know we are not perfect, it follows that we are also not righteous. In order to get into heaven, our righteousness needs to come from someone or something outside ourselves. That someone is Jesus Christ—"Him who knew no sin." The perfection of God in Jesus is imputed (ascribed) to us by virtue of His character. We need His perfection because our sin separates us from God. When we believe, the righteousness of Jesus is given to us to make us right before God. This is the divine exchange. Another way of speaking about this is Jesus is our penal substitute who bore the penalty for our sins. This has been the most popular understanding among Protestants, building upon Anselm's satisfaction theory.

The act of exchange involves giving one thing and receiving another. In Romans 5:12–21, Paul explains how Jesus Christ is God's provision for our justification when our participatory response is the obedience of faith and not the bondage of legalism. In other words, God provides Jesus Christ in exchange for our obedience of faith in the context of covenant relationship. Theologian Dale Moody writes on this divine exchange that it is "a subjective response *through* faith in obedience to Jesus Christ as Lord in order to experience the blessings of the objective justification by grace that triumphs over sin. . . . Where there is no human obedience in faith there is no justification by grace."[1] Moody also points out the importance of covenant relation as an aspect of the divine exchange. "Old Testament studies have shown beyond much doubt that this righteous relation is obedience to the covenant relation. The faithfulness of God calls for the faithfulness of man."[2]

There is a difference between "having" something and "becoming" something. God's righteousness doesn't just cover us like an overcoat, hiding our true, sinful nature. His righteousness changes us from the inside out. Because of His power working in us, each one of us becomes the righteousness of God in Christ.

The finished work of the cross means that you and I can now live in the fulfillment of Joel's Old Testament prophecy: "And it shall come to pass afterward that I will pour out My Spirit on all flesh; your sons and your daughters shall prophesy, your old men shall dream dreams, your young men shall see visions" (Joel 2:28 NKJV).

What we are privileged to experience is something the Old Testament prophets, priests, and kings could have only dreamed of. They were able to experience the presence of the Holy Spirit as He rested upon them; but you and I get to experience the fullness of the Holy Spirit as He dwells within us. In Paul's letter to the Colossians, he said, "To them God has chosen to make known among the Gentiles the glorious riches of this mystery, which is Christ in you, the hope of glory" (Col. 1:27).

It is God's great pleasure to give everyone (who believes) His magnificent presence as "Christ in us" manifesting in the power of His Spirit. The Holy Spirit living in you gives you everything you need, everything required for righteous, holy living in the presence of God. When you receive Jesus, you are now the righteousness of Christ. Jesus is our assured hope of glory, and we must steward well this great gift, living faithfully unto death.

IF JESUS WERE STILL ALIVE . . .

Imagine for a moment that Jesus had never died. The implications are staggering. We would have no communication with God. We would be without access to Him, because the veil that grants access to His presence would never have been "torn in two from top to bottom" (Matt. 27:51). We would be unable to "come boldly to the throne of grace" (Heb. 4:16 NKJV), because our sin would not be allowed in His presence.

If Jesus had never died, the eternal implications would be even worse. Without the blood of Jesus Christ covering our sin, we would be shut out from heaven. We would have no way of getting our spirit from this earth into heaven with God. When Jesus died, He went to "prepare a place for [us]" (John 14:3). He made a path for us to heaven so that where He has gone, we can follow!

If Jesus had never died, your ministry to others would be lifeless. There would have been no "sound from heaven, as of a rushing mighty wind" (Acts 2:2 NKJV) as the Holy Spirit came to baptize the disciples gathered in the Upper Room. There would be no "tongues, as the Spirit gave them utterance" (Acts 2:4 NKJV). There would be no "power from on high" (Luke 24:49 NKJV) in your prayers. This is why Jesus said, "It is to your advantage that I go away; for if I do not go away, the Helper will not come to you; but if I depart, I will send Him to you" (John 16:7 NKJV). You owe every ounce of transformation in your life to the work of the Holy Spirit.

Without the cross of Jesus Christ, the Spirit of Jesus could have never "come to you." Without the cross, God would be distant, accessible only through other people.[3] Yet because of the cross of Jesus Christ, the Holy Spirit dwells "in your hearts through faith" (Eph. 3:17 NKJV). Because Jesus Christ came and died in the flesh, our Father in heaven can now make a home inside our hearts. It is for this reason that when the Pharisees asked Jesus "when the kingdom of God would come," He replied, "The kingdom of God does not come with observation; nor will they say, 'See here!' or 'See there!' For indeed, the kingdom of God is within you" (Luke 17:20–21 NKJV).

DIVINE TRANSFORMATION

As the kingdom of God comes within you, a divine transformation takes place that is both instantaneous and progressive. At the very moment you put your trust in Jesus Christ as Lord and Savior, you are made holy, sanctified. This is the first aspect of the sanctification process. The apostle Paul put it thus,

> As for us, we can't help but thank God for you, dear brothers and sisters loved by the Lord. We are always thankful that God chose you to be

among the first to experience salvation—a salvation that came through the Spirit who makes you holy and through your belief in the truth. (2 Thess. 2:13 NLT)

To be "sanctified" means to be consecrated or purified:[4] to have your heart and life transformed by the power of God. Sanctification is instantaneous; God gives you a new heart, and He puts His Spirit within you, fulfilling Ezekiel's prophecy:

I will give you a new heart and put a new spirit within you; I will take the heart of stone out of your flesh and give you a heart of flesh. I will put My Spirit within you and cause you to walk in My statutes, and you will keep My judgments and do them. (Ezek. 36:26–27 NKJV)

As you'll recall from chapter 4, my own moment of sanctification was followed by a circuitous process that involved occasions where I slid back into my old ways only to take hold of the grace of God and allow my mind to be further renewed, until I reached a point at which I was able to stand in the power of His Spirit against my flesh. That process continues to this day. Do I struggle with the same issues that beset me as a young man? No. However, I have enough wisdom from God to know that my own sinful nature will not be fully put to rest until that day when I meet Jesus face-to-face. Until then, I will gladly live in the progression of my heart toward the prize.

The apostle Paul was himself also familiar with this process.

Brothers, I do not consider myself yet to have laid hold of it. But one thing I do: Forgetting what is behind and straining toward what is ahead, I press on toward the goal to win the prize of God's heavenly calling in Christ Jesus. All of us who are mature should embrace this point of view. And if you think differently about some issue, God will reveal this to you as well. (Phil. 3:13–15 BSB)

Our initial sanctification is followed by progressive growth and renewal as our mind is conformed more and more to the mind of Christ through His Spirit living within us. "And do not be conformed to this world, but be transformed by the renewing of your mind, that you may prove what is that good and acceptable and perfect will of God" (Rom. 12:2 NKJV). Think of this progressive process of sanctification as synergistic—the inner-working of God in you by His mighty gift of grace.

The writer of Hebrews presented this mystery well: "For by one offering He has perfected forever those who are being sanctified" (Heb. 10:14 NKJV). Not only do you now have an invitation to live a life of holiness and righteousness, but God will actually "enable you" to keep His Word if you let Him.

Jesus already served as our sacrifice once for all; but now it is our responsibility to present ourselves as a living sacrifice to God every single day, to refuse to allow the temptations of this world to entangle us, and instead be renewed by the Spirit of God. We are to deny ourselves and take up our cross daily as we follow Jesus.

God isn't interested in behavior modification. We can't change our self from the outside in. God wants heart transformation, which means allowing Him to change you from the inside out. This is the difference between law and grace. The old covenant law says that one must work to become holy to please God. New Testament grace says that one must receive the holiness that Jesus Christ already died for us to have. God is after your interior. He wants your heart. His change takes time and a willingness to submit to the process in obedience and sacrifice.

In the same way, God has deposited something in us that causes us to rise to the holiness He has prescribed for us. "Having believed, you were sealed with the Holy Spirit of promise, who is the guarantee" (Eph. 1:13–14 NKJV). God has already given His word that you will rise to the destiny He has laid out for you. His work in you will be evidence of change that 1) you cannot deny, and 2) everyone around you cannot ignore.

FOLLOW JESUS

Jesus is our perfect model for godly living. During His time on earth He showed by example what it looks like to only do what He heard the Father doing, only say what He heard the Father saying. When the religious authorities asked Him why He healed on the Sabbath, He replied, "My Father is still working, and I also am working" (John 5:17 NRSV). Then He went on to explain to them the authority of the Son.

> Jesus said to them, "Very truly, I tell you, the Son can do nothing on his own, but only what he sees the Father doing; for whatever the Father does, the Son does likewise. The Father loves the Son and shows him all that he himself is doing; and he will show him greater works than these, so that you will be astonished." (vv. 19–20 NRSV)

The "greater works" Jesus was referring to are the resurrection and our salvation, and all that goes along with it that was to come about from the finished work of the cross.

In answer to Pilate's question of why Jesus had to die, Scripture says that Jesus died so that we might become the righteousness of God. When Jesus asks us to lay down our lives for Him, He isn't asking something of us that He hasn't already done. He has gone before us and made a way for us so that we can follow. You see, once you know something is possible, your perspective is forever changed. Jesus broke the barrier and we can follow

Him. Yes, we can marvel at all He has done, but ultimately we are called to follow Him. God has declared you worthy of the cross of Jesus Christ. In response, you must declare that Jesus is worthy of your life laid at His feet.

"Most assuredly, I say to you, he who believes in Me, the works that I do he will do also; and greater works than these he will do, because I go to My Father" (John 14:12 NKJV).

fourteen

JESUS DIED SO THAT WE MIGHT BE RECONCILED TO THE FATHER

Once you were alienated from God and were hostile in your
minds because of your evil deeds. But now He has reconciled
you by Christ's physical body through death to present you holy,
unblemished, and blameless in His presence—if indeed you
continue in your faith, established and firm, not moved from the
hope of the gospel you heard . . .
—COLOSSIANS 1:21–23 BSB

Jesus died in order that we might be reconciled to God. But how are we to understand this reconciliation? Was Jesus reconciling the Father to us, or was the Father in Jesus reconciling us to Himself? In his book *The Word of Truth*, Dr. Dale Moody, my Baptist professor for systematic theology, quoted Scottish theogian James Denny, who said,

When reconciliation is spoken of in St. Paul, the subject is always God, and the object is always man. The work of reconciling is one in which the initiative is taken by God, and the cost is borne by Him; men are reconciled in the passive, or allow themselves to be reconciled or receive the reconciliation. We never read that God has been reconciled. God does the work of reconciliation in or through Christ, and especially through his death.[1]

Moody continued, "God as the source did not reconcile himself but us to himself through Christ. . . . Our reconciliation is to be continuous and conditional because 'participation depends upon a continuation in the faith (Col. 1:22–23a).'"[2]

In the book of Romans, Paul addressed reconciliation as the act of making a person consistent with God as a transaction that begins through the cross and is ongoing.

> Therefore, since we have now been justified by His blood, how much more shall we be saved from wrath through Him! For if, when we were enemies of God, we were reconciled to Him through the death of His Son, how much more, having been reconciled, shall we be saved through His life! Not only that, but we also rejoice in God through our Lord Jesus Christ, through whom we have now received reconciliation. (Rom. 5:9–11 bsb)

THE POWER OF THE GOSPEL

It is important to note the problem here is the hostility of humans toward God—we were His enemies; He was not our enemy. Reconciliation was made possible through the death of Jesus while we were yet sinners and enemies of God, hostile to Him. However, having been reconciled to God by the death of Jesus, we shall be saved by the life of Jesus. I believe Paul's phrase "saved through His life" (v. 10 BSB) is a reference to Jesus' continuing work as our great High Priest and His work as our advocate.

Some streams of the church emphasize more Jesus' whole life—His incarnation, His teachings, His example of how we are to live, and His death, resurrection, and ascension—as being important to our salvation. As important as all this is, it seems that salvation through His life is referring to our present state *after* having been reconciled—not limited to His ongoing roles as the great High Priest and Advocate, but also His living in us via the Holy Spirit. We are now a new creation, born of the Holy Spirit, living in the Spirit, walking by the Spirit, not the Law, with the power and the energy of His life enabling us to labor or work and live victoriously over sin rather than slavishly bound to sin.

It helps to think of reconciliation as the initial act that removes our guilt and begins the ongoing process of sanctification. This is the power of the gospel, a gospel that reconciles us to God, gives us access to God, and makes available the empowerment of God through power imparted into the believer by the Holy Spirit whereby the weak are made strong.

Let me take you back to Mozambique, to share more with you about my friends Rolland and Heidi Baker. It is through the Bakers that I so often see the power of God to forgive, reconcile, and change character. Mozambique is a country ravaged by civil war and the resulting poverty that crushes the people. Scores are living in tents and abandoned buildings, cooking outside over charcoal fires, with only a single piece of clothing—a filthy, tattered rag to cover their bodies. Heidi regularly visits the poorest of the poor. She is an amazing ambassador of reconciliation for Christ.

I went with Heidi and her team one evening to visit the poor as she shared about Jesus and incarnated His love through her words and actions. The people were so honored to host a visit from Heidi that they shared their dinner with her—boiled cat. After our meal, Heidi began to move among the people where she encountered a young woman with a terrible discharge who desperately needed antibiotics. Heidi arranged for her to be taken to a clinic and treated. With Heidi, it is always about stopping for the one.

The team that assists Heidi on these outreaches is made up primarily of abandoned children she has found on the streets. As they experience the living gospel through Heidi and Rolland, they are reconciled to God and eventually become her evangelists, sharing and demonstrating God's love to the broken. In a place like Mozambique, where the needs are so great, it seems that everyone is open and interested in the gospel. Former street children pray for the sick and needy, and many are healed and accept Jesus as their Savior.

One day, I met a young man who had come to Heidi from the streets as a small boy. Despite the love lavished upon him, for years he seemed incorrigible. He would repeatedly steal from Heidi and her family, break the rules, and return to the streets. Many encouraged her to give up on him, but Heidi refused, firmly believing in the power of love to undo the damage of the nightmarish life he had lived.

This troubled boy grew into a young man. One day he was with Heidi as she ministered in a remote village. The people there embraced another religion, and as Heidi shared the gospel, they became angry and began to throw stones at her and her team. That is when this incorrigible young man ran to Heidi and stood in front of her to shield her from the stones with his own body. Love won in his life. The incorrigible became the encourager and the defender.

NEW LIFE IN CHRIST

There are two aspects of reconciliation—forgiveness of sins and being made alive with new life. This "new life" is not a reference to the final resurrection. It is an experience that does not have to wait until the return of Jesus. It is a present reality made available to us now, as we live, through the cross. It is a new quality of life so different from our former life that it is compared to being dead and then experiencing life—new life that brings with it the power to live as overcomers.

This new life, which begins with the initial act of reconciliation, is nowhere more evident than in the Village of Joy in Mozambique, where many of the children Heidi rescues from the streets come to live. Most of these children have endured horrendous abuse and violence. They have been beaten, prostituted, abandoned, and starved. Some have witnessed atrocities beyond our worst imagination, such as their parents and families being slaughtered in front of them. They carry enormous trauma that would normally take years of counseling to bring even the smallest measure of healing. Yet, after living in the Village of Joy, they become emotionally and mentally healthy, happy children. A group of psychiatrists became intrigued by this and came to study what Heidi was doing with the children.

How are these children healed? Heidi will tell you it is the power of the gospel that heals them. She raises them in the power of the gospel in the love of Christ. The inner healing and deliverance that occurs in these young children in the presence of the Holy Spirit is miraculous. They are taught a different value system from the one that was imposed upon them by the world.

Heidi starts by educating the children in order to give them the opportunity to become future leaders in Mozambique—leaders who have integrity, who love people. Years ago, she started an elementary school on the base, then a secondary school. Today she is starting a university to train doctors, lawyers, and engineers. Recently, Heidi sent five of these adult children from the Iris School on scholarship to Stanford University's summer program because she knows that it is through educated leaders that nations rise up out of poverty and violence.

In answer to Pilate's question of why Jesus had to die, Scripture says that Jesus died so that we might be reconciled to God. Former prostitutes lead worship, those who were once thieves are now encouragers and defenders, and those without hope of education are now taking their place as educated leaders who lead by example, full of the love of God for their people and their God. A broken people are being reconciled to God through the love of God in His matchless Son, Jesus, enjoying the benefits of reconciliation for believers.

"For he has rescued us from the dominion of darkness and brought us into the kingdom of the Son he loves, in whom we have redemption, the forgiveness of sins" (Col. 1:13–14).

fifteen

JESUS DIED TO BECOME OUR MODEL AND PROPHET

Throughout Church history Jesus has been described by three offices that He fulfilled: prophet, priest, and king. The Son of God clothed Himself in human flesh in order to reveal the Father to us. He came to open up a way of grace to deal with our sins. He took on our flesh and entered into humanity in order that we humans could receive the Spirit of God and take on deity. The theology of atonement that pertains to humankind being made divine through solidarity with the work of Jesus on the cross is known as the recapitulation theory of the atonement. According to recapitulation theology, Jesus is the new Adam who succeeds where the old Adam failed. Therefore, we are able to partake of the divine nature that was not available to us before the cross. The apostle Paul put it thus: "And because of his glory and excellence, he has given us great and precious promises. These are the promises that enable you to share his divine nature and escape the world's corruption caused by human desires" (2 Peter 1:4 NLT). He came as a lamb that would also be a lion. He came as a servant but would become the ruler until the Father had placed all other authorities, powers, and rulers "under His feet." He came as the Son of Man who would be glorified and worshiped as the King of kings and Lord of lords, the Son of God.

In chapters 3 through 7 we examined this aspect of Jesus ruling as conquering King. Jesus, by His power, has overcome the devil and his demons; destroyed captivity, drugs, and other addictions; destroyed diseases and death itself; and disarmed the powers and authorities. He has deceived the deceiver, who believed he could destroy the Son of God at the cross in his human weakness, not realizing that Jesus would be raised by the power of God and in this way would bind the strong man (the devil) and be able to plunder his kingdom—the earth. The Lamb that was slain has become the Lion of Judah, making a public spectacle of the devil.

Jesus also fulfills the office of priest, more exactly the great High Priest. As we've examined Jesus' priestly work, we've seen that He established the new covenant and became our great High Priest, opening up the way for us to come confidently to the throne of grace that we may receive mercy and help in our times of need. In His priestly role, Jesus made forgiveness possible, eternal life an assurance for His followers, and the new covenant a reality when we are born again and filled or baptized with, in, and by the Holy Spirit. As the High Priest who offers His own life as the sacrifice, Jesus establishes and reveals the righteousness and justice and holiness of God and reconciles us to the Father. He reveals the grace of God—and the Father was in Jesus reconciling the world unto Himself.

In this chapter we will consider two major perspectives regarding Jesus and the cross: Jesus as the model and Jesus' death understood as moral influence. We will look at both in relationship to the office of prophet that Jesus fulfilled. Jesus, like some Old Testament prophets before Him, condemned outward religious acts that were not from the heart. He called people to the new covenant, which surpassed the old covenant. He pointed them to the need of the promise of the Father—the baptism with the Holy Spirit. He came as the Prophet to reveal the way, the truth, and the life, even as He Himself was the revelation of these things. As the Prophet, He points to justice and mercy, calling people to see Him in the poor and marginalized—that what we do to them we do also to Him. As Prophet He strongly calls people to obedience, linking love for God as expressed through obedience to God. As Prophet He comes to have an impact upon human devotion to God by revealing to us that there was a moral influence in His life. When He asks us to follow Him, it is a daily denial of self that requires us to enter into discipleship that includes suffering for Him—carrying our cross.

As Prophet, Jesus modeled by His life what it means to walk in faith and in obedience to the Father, what it is like to live by the Spirit. Because Jesus the Son in His prophetic office reveals to humanity what the Father is like, it is possible to know how to live in such a way that we imitate God. As the Prophet, He calls people to follow Him. Jesus told Thomas, "If you really know me, you will know my Father as well" (John 14:7). The apostle Paul would ask the people of his churches to imitate him because he believed he was imitating Christ. He also wrote to the Ephesians, "Therefore be imitators of God, as beloved children" (Eph. 5:1 NASB). In 1 Thessalonians 1:6 Paul mentioned imitating again: "You also became imitators of us and of the Lord" (NASB).

As the Prophet, Jesus announced the good news that God's kingdom was at hand. John 14:12 records the following important words of Jesus: "Truly, truly, I say to you, he who believes in me will also do the works that I do; and greater works than these will he do, because I go to the Father" (RSV). These words imply a similarity between the works of Jesus and our works. In this context "the works" refer to the signs and wonders, healing and miracles. Mark 16 has a similar implication for similarity between Jesus' life and ours. Jesus said, "And these signs will accompany those who believe: in my name they will cast out demons; they will speak in new tongues; they will pick up serpents with their hands; and if they drink any deadly poison, it will not hurt them; they will lay their hands on the sick, and they will recover" (vv. 17–18 ESV). All of these passages relate to the possibility for believers to follow Jesus' example in the realm of supernatural signs and wonders—healings, miracles, and power over demons. This is the New Testament understanding of discipleship. We need to change the way we think about the possibilities and realities of life.

HOW DO WE UNDERSTAND
JESUS AS OUR MODEL?

Jon Ruthven has pointed out that in the first-century Jewish world the disciples of a rabbi were not satisfied to know the teachings of their master teacher. They wanted to follow his example in their lifestyles as well. When this is applied to New Testament believers, it means Jesus is to be our model not only in ethics but also in advancing the kingdom of God through the power of God.[1] The question is, "How are we to understand Jesus as our model?" There are two answers to that question.

The first answer is, Jesus did supernatural acts—the healings, miracles, and deliverances—in His deity while the normal aspects of His life were done in His humanity. This was the position of the Sixth Ecumenical Council, the Third Council of Constantinople (680–681). This position is the official position of Roman Catholicism. Most Protestants don't hold this council as authoritative in their lives and churches, while many Charismatics and Pentecostals have rejected this position for what is called the kenotic answer, which is the second answer to the question, "How do we understand Jesus as our model?"

The kenotic answer is based upon Philippians 2:5–11 and the word *kenosis*, which means "self-emptying." This answer to how Jesus did what He did is also supported by Jesus' statements in John 5:19, 30. He did the healings and miracles, the signs and wonders, in His humanity, choosing not to do anything in His deity so that He could be the pioneer of our faith. In this way He was able to model the Christian life. This model emphasizes our ability to follow Jesus in discipleship, doing what He did, even doing the "greater things." The ability to do such miraculous acts is through the Holy Spirit. Paul is also our example. In Colossians he wrote, "To this end I strenuously contend with all the energy Christ so powerfully works in me" (Col. 1:29). It is with God's energy, not our own power, that we labor. His energy works powerfully in us, enabling the greater things to be done in His name.

These two answers to the question "How are we to understand Jesus as our model?" might at first seem to be contradictory. The first answer says that Jesus did these miraculous works in His deity, while the second one says He did them in His humanity, dependent upon the Holy Spirit. How do these two answers impact our ability to follow Jesus and obey His commandments to heal and deliver? I want to begin with the second answer. Jesus is my model because He did His miracles in His humanity through the power of the Holy Spirit. This kenotic understanding of Jesus has been my personal view since 1984, when I was first touched powerfully by the Holy Spirit. I have taught this perspective all over the world and in most of my books. However, while preparing to teach a seminary course on Christian theologies for Global Awakening Theological Seminary, I discovered the position of the Sixth Ecumenical Council.

The official position of the Sixth Ecumenical Council rejected the kenotic understanding that Jesus did not do His miracles in and through His deity, but in His humanity. Instead, the council's conclusion was, "Christ had two natures and two activities: as God, working miracles, rising from the dead and ascending into heaven; as Man, performing the ordinary acts of daily life. Each nature exercises its own free will."[2] As I mentioned before, this particular council has not been accepted as binding by most Protestant denominations and other groups within the ancient church, but it was the accepted position within the Catholic and Orthodox Churches.

Given that many Christians will accept as the truth this official position of the council concerning the miraculous works of Jesus, one could ask, "How is Jesus still able to be our model since, by this council's understanding, Jesus didn't work miracles dependent upon the Holy Spirit, but through His own deity?" The answer is found in the truth of the new covenant. As Jesus became human to redeem, in so doing, He made it possible for humans to take deity into our lives in the power of the Holy Spirit. The Holy Spirit comes into us, resides in us, lives with us, empowers us, changes us, and conforms us to His image. The greater things that we do are not done in or by or through our flesh. Rather, they are done through the deity we carry within us. The signs and wonders, miracles and healings are done in, by, and through the Holy Spirit. In the incarnation, Jesus took on our flesh, but in the new birth and the baptism in the Spirit, our flesh takes into itself the Holy Spirit who is God, the third person of the Trinity.

The difference in the two answers to the question is this: if Jesus did what He did in His humanity, by the Holy Spirit, He *is* our model. We, too, do the supernatural things He told us to do by the power of the same Holy Spirit. If Jesus did what He did in His divinity, then He is still our model because of the new birth we experience when we become believers. When we are born again, we take on the supernatural power of God, which resides in us by the Holy Spirit. We are no longer mere mortals, devoid of supernatural power. His incarnation has made possible the beginning of our deification, a process that will culminate in the consummation when Jesus returns. Until then the power of God by the Holy Spirit works in and through us. In that sense we are not accomplishing anything in or by our natural selves. Instead, what is being done through our lives is being done by the Holy Spirit that is now part of our nature, bringing about a new nature, one empowered by the Holy Spirit in us.

In Christ we have both access to the throne where Jesus is seated as our High Priest and intercessor, and we have empowerment by the grace of God. His grace provides the access to the throne and is the basis for the empowerment from the throne. It is this empowerment from the throne that enables us to co-labor with Christ as part of the plan of salvation. Jesus didn't die only to provide us eternal life to take us to heaven. He died to bring the power of heaven to us, to enable us to advance the rule of the kingdom of God on the earth.

Whether one holds to the Orthodox position of the Sixth Ecumenical Council or the kenotic view of Jesus' incarnation, the followers of Jesus are still enabled to follow Him, to work with Him in the realm of the supernatural because of the supernatural power of the Holy Spirit. Paul wrote of this kind of supernatural discipleship in several of his letters. The appendix in this book gives reference to the oldest English translations in chronological order. I have included this because it is important to gain insight into when the word *preached* was first introduced into the translation of Romans 15:19. The main point of all this—whether one agrees with the Sixth Ecumenical Council or the kenotic understanding of the incarnation—is that as believers we still have a basis for understanding discipleship as including our responsibility and ability to experience signs and wonders, healings and miracles in our lives because God lives inside of us via the Holy Spirit. This is not a weak form of God, but *is* God, and God in us can do God things through us. It is not us doing God things in our humanity, but God doing God things through us by the power of His energy that works so mightily through us.

JESUS' CROSS AND ITS POWER FOR MORAL INFLUENCE (JESUS THE PROPHET)

There was an expectation that one of the aspects of the Messiah would be his role as a prophet—the prophet God would raise up like unto Moses. Prophets in the Old Testament were primarily calling the people of God back to faithfulness to the covenant. Instead of receiving the law on Mount Sinai, Jesus as Prophet gives us a more profound covenant relationship with deeper obedience that deals with heart attitudes, not just outward compliance. It is a covenant not from the mouth, but from the heart.

Jesus' teachings were deeply rooted in Old Testament prophetic tradition. Of the thirty times the prophets are quoted in the New Testament, nineteen of them are from Jesus. He quoted from Jeremiah, Daniel, Zechariah, Hosea, and Malachi. Yet, His favorite prophet seems to have been Isaiah. Like the prophets Hosea and Amos, Jesus identified with the poor and desired mercy instead of sacrifice. He identified with the prisoners, the hungry, and the naked. He spoke often about the value of women and children, particularly in the gospel of Luke.

It is from the life and teachings of Jesus that Christianity has developed a profound ministry to the sick not only through healing prayers, but also by establishing the first hospitals of the Western world, the first hospices, and through the giving of alms to the poor. In fact, Christian philanthropy was known throughout the ancient world. I lived for sixteen years in the St. Louis area, where almost all the hospitals had been started by Christians. The majority were Catholic hospitals, but other denominations had their hospitals as well. Even in America, most of the first colleges in this country were created by Christian denominations. Establishing educational institutions, giving alms to the poor, building hospitals and hospices, and a multitude of other philanthropic activities have characterized the Christian church and its message for twenty centuries now.

SOCIAL ASPECTS OF THE GOSPEL

However, it was in the twentieth century that we saw the birth of a deeper understanding of poverty and evil. There arose men and women of an evangelical nature who had been deeply touched by God. They raised the issue of the social aspects of the gospel and championed the causes of labor by preaching on the importance of the unionization of labor to help alleviate the cause of poverty—the exploitation of workers by a form of capitalism that had lost its conscience. This social gospel was propelled by an understanding of the kingdom of God: that this kingdom wasn't put off until the millennium or the renewed heaven and earth. It was an understanding that the kingdom of God was already at work in the earth and had ethical concerns not just for the poor but for the conditions that were causing such poverty.

Men like Washington Gladden, a Congregationalist pastor, championed the application of Christian law to social needs. He was not championing socialism or laissez faire economics. He was the first well-known Protestant pastor to champion unionization of labor. His book *Working People and Their Employers* was published in 1876. He has been considered the father of the social gospel. His second book, *The Christian Way: Whither It Leads and How to Go On*, was published in 1877. It is hard to believe, but this was considered by some to be the first call in America for everyday life to be influenced by Christian values. He fought for Christian values to be applied to secular institutions. Like his successor, Gladden had a profound experience of God in his life, but he developed a liberal theology.

Walter Rauschenbusch, a Baptist, would be the second most famous person in the development of the social gospel. His experience as a young pastor ministering in Hell's Kitchen in New York City caused him to seek to go past the philanthropy of the church to deal with the issues that were causing the dire living conditions of the poor. The situation was so bad that he was called upon to conduct funeral after funeral for children who had died due to the unsanitary condition of their tenant quarters and from overwork in factories. There were no child labor laws at the time, no forty-hour workweek, no overtime pay, no OSHA to make sure the working conditions were safe. Women and children were worked hard and not paid as much as men.

Rauschenbusch was propelled into the social gospel by what he had seen and experienced and as such was considered one of the fathers of the movement, perhaps the most influential. He wrote five important books in ten years, from 1907 to 1917: *Christianity and the Social Crisis* (1907), *Christianizing the Social Order* (1912), *Dare We Be Christians* (1914), *The Social Principles of Jesus* (1916), and *A Theology for the Social Gospel* (1917). Mark Galli wrote, "Martin Luther King Jr. said of Rauschenbusch, 'His writings left an indelible imprint on my thinking,' and his understanding of the Kingdom of God continues to appeal to those who want to combine evangelical passion with social justice."[3]

JESUS GAVE US A GOSPEL THAT IS BOTH SOCIAL AND PERSONAL

Grave social issues were raised during the nineteenth and twentieth centuries by the Industrial Age that brought about urbanization of the population. It was during this time that a great increase of immigration was occurring. In response to these concerns, a movement that politically would be considered progressive was birthed within Protestantism that attempted to deal with these issues—developing a theology from the Bible, especially the Old Testament prophets and Jesus' moral teachings, with the intent of focusing God's concern and the gospel upon the social needs of oppressed workers, legal immigrants, and the marginalized. Because this movement prioritized social salvation over personal salvation, it became divisive. Fundamentalists believed the gospel was being truncated. The truth is, when the gospel only has either personal or social implications, it *is* truncated. The gospel must speak to both the personal and the social, not pit them against each other.

The weakness of the social gospel was in its attempt to bring social implications to the message of Jesus, the prophets of the Old Testament, and the implications of the kingdom of God. It did this by attacking the understanding of the gospel that had primarily a personal concern for the salvation of people's souls. The kingdom of God has both social and personal concerns. The gospel of the kingdom involves the concerns of liberals like Gladden, Rauschenbusch, and Harry Emerson Fosdick; and those of fundamentalists like D. L. Moody, R. A. Torrey, Clarence E. Macartney, and J. Gresham Machen. The gospel is both social and personal.

One example of how to balance social and personal aspects of the gospel is found in the ministry of the late apostle Ben Smith of Deliverance Evangelistic Church in Philadelphia, Pennsylvania. When the liberal seminaries wanted to send students to see a church that was instrumental in social ministry and social redemption, they sent them to Deliverance Evangelistic Church, a ten-thousand-member African American church. The church bought property to build businesses for black individuals and had many social programs to better the lives of the people of the community. However, it was not liberal theologically. Deliverance Evangelistic Church believed in deliverance from demons, physical healing in Jesus' name, and a strong evangelistic outreach to the streets, and as such they were a model of both the social and personal aspects of the gospel.

Another outstanding example of reuniting the social and personal aspects of the gospel is found in Iris Global Ministries in Mozambique, which Rolland and Heidi Baker founded. Years ago, when I first went to Mozambique to work for a short time with Rolland and Heidi, they shared their vision, which was to affect the nation of Mozambique. They were not only feeding and clothing the poor, building houses for widows and caring for children, and digging water wells; they were also casting out demons, healing the sick, and restoring sight to the blind and hearing to the deaf. In fact, almost all the deaf Heidi prayed for in Mozambique were receiving healing, and the dead were occasionally being raised.

Iris Global Ministries is a great example of how both the personal and social aspects of the gospel can be fulfilled. The gospel of Jesus is a wholistic gospel, not a bifurcated one. Rolland and Heidi want to represent Jesus to the people of Mozambique because they believe the love of Christ "looks like something."

I believe as we look toward the future we are going to see an ecumenism of the Spirit in the church, where greater numbers of healings and miracles and expressions of the gifts of the Spirit exist alongside a greater concern for the social implications of the gospel. I believe we will see an acceptance of the belief in the *powers* influencing social structures for evil purposes, and at the same time the acceptance of real *demons* influencing the lives of individuals.[4]

In answer to Pilate's question of why Jesus had to die, Scripture teaches that Jesus lived and died as both fully God and fully man to model how we are to live out the gospel.

sixteen

JESUS DIED TO FULFILL
GOD'S ORIGINAL PLAN

A study of the Bible reveals several hundred Old Testament scriptures that point to Jesus, and that were, in fact, fulfilled by Jesus in His lifetime, as reflected in the New Testament. My purpose here is not to examine all of those. However, we are going to look at a number of places in Scripture that clearly show Jesus as the One spoken of and foreshadowed in the Old Testament as the Christ, the Messiah, with a focus on the purposeful obedience of Jesus to give His life to bring about the new covenant.

It is important to understand that none of what happened to Jesus was a surprise to either the Father or the Son. Jesus was not a radical end-times preacher who expected the kingdom to come at any moment. He was not surprised by His rejection. He was not trapped by His ethical preaching resulting in His crucifixion. No, as He told Peter, He could have asked His Father, who would have sent twelve legions of angels to deliver Him. Remember, only one angel was needed to break the power of the most powerful army in the world at the time—Pharaoh's army in Egypt—when God brought the Hebrew children out of captivity.

The passion of Christ was not a situation that had grown out of hand

and taken Jesus by surprise. Peter's impassioned sermon on Pentecost gives voice to the reality that Jesus was handed over to the Jews by God's set purpose and foreknowledge:

> Fellow Israelites, listen to this: Jesus of Nazareth was a man accredited by God to you by miracles, wonders and signs, which God did among you through him, as you yourselves know. *This man was handed over to you by God's deliberate plan and foreknowledge;* and you, with the help of wicked men, put him to death by nailing him to the cross. But God raised him from the dead, freeing him from the agony of death, because it was impossible for death to keep its hold on him. (Acts 2:22–24, emphasis mine)

In the Gospels we find Jesus teaching His disciples in preparation for the cross (Luke 9:22, 30–32), with His face set toward Jerusalem (Luke 9:51–53). He was not surprised by the suffering that was soon to come upon Him. He had seen crucifixion and knew how terrible a death it was. "He then began to teach them that the Son of Man must suffer many things and be rejected by the elders, the chief priests and the teachers of the law, and that he must be killed and after three days rise again" (Mark 8:31).

When Peter heard this teaching, he rashly rebuked Jesus only to be rebuked in turn by Jesus. "He spoke plainly about this, and Peter took him aside and began to rebuke him. But when Jesus turned and looked at his disciples, he rebuked Peter. 'Get behind me, Satan!' he said. 'You do not have in mind the concerns of God, but merely human concerns'" (vv. 32–33). Jesus knew it was the Father's will for Him to embrace the cross for us, and that it was Satan's intention to dissuade Him from the cross.

On the night before His crucifixion, Jesus gathered His beloved disciples together for a meal. Much happened around the table that night. What was lost in the garden was about to be restored on the cross. But first came the meal. The betrayer was released, the denier was identified, and the Lamb of God revealed. And a most glorious invitation was issued—"Come gather together around the table often and remember the sacrifice of My body and blood as you eat the bread and drink the wine."[1]

The Lamb of God, slain before the foundations of the world for the redemption of humankind, sat with His closest companions on the night before His greatest agony and found comfort at the table. Jesus knew the time had come for Him to leave this world and go to the Father (John 13:1), with the knowledge that God had given all things into His hands, and that He who had come from God was going to God (John 13:3).

One can only imagine the depth of His suffering. In His "now and not yet" state, fully God and fully man, Jesus knew the crushing weight of the sin of all humankind. It drove Him to His knees in the garden, there in the midst of His beloved disciples. Yet He went to the cross for the joy set before Him, fully aware that in the fullness of time we would all sit together again at the great banquet table for the magnificent marriage supper of the Lamb.

All of this took place in God's perfect timing, which for Jesus in the flesh was during Passover. Jesus came to Jerusalem during the Passover festival to become the Passover Lamb of God. His timing wasn't chance or luck. He knew exactly where He was going and what He was going to do. Imagine the scene in Jerusalem, as Jews come from near and far to the holy city to celebrate Pesach, or the Festival of Unleavened Bread, in commemoration of the exodus. Historical estimates place the population in and around Jerusalem at somewhere near twenty to thirty thousand at the time Jesus arrived there for the Passover and His Passion. This number would swell when one hundred fifty thousand people streamed into Jerusalem to celebrate the Passover at that time.[2]

In accordance with custom, the main focus of the Passover festival was the sacrifice of the Paschal lamb. Every Jew was required to eat of a young lamb sacrificed in the temple. People would gather in groups or in families to eat the sacrifice together, along with unleavened bread and bitter herbs. The entire lamb had to be eaten with no bones broken. As Scripture tells us, Jesus hung on the cross in His entirety, and none of His bones were broken during or after the crucifixion (John 19:36; Ex. 12:43–46; Ps. 34:19–20).

Jesus not only symbolizes the Old Testament sacrificial lamb; He symbolizes the entire Old Testament sacrificial system with its priests continually making sacrifices in the temple to atone for the sins of the people. Jesus is our perfect sacrifice and our great High Priest. We are now the temple, and Jesus has come to reside in us. Daily sacrifices are no longer necessary because Jesus is our once-and-for-all sacrifice. Moses prophesied in Deuteronomy 18:15–22 that a prophet would come after him who would be greater than him. That prophet is Jesus. The imperfect judges in the book of Judges who deliver God's people are but a shadow of the once-and-for-all sacrifice Judge and Deliverer, Jesus Christ, who will judge and deliver the people of God.

Fast-forward to the book of Isaiah and you will find an abundance of Jesus there. In chapter 11, the prophet spoke of the child to be born who would rule the earth from the throne of David and establish His kingdom with justice and righteousness forevermore. Luke 1:32–33 and 3:21–23 echo these verses from Isaiah. Both Isaiah 11:10 and 53:2 speak of the Messiah as the root that will come from the stump of Jesse. As both fully God and fully man, Scripture tells us that Jesus had His human origin from the line of David, with Jesse being King David's father, and His godly origin from the action of the Holy Spirit on a virgin, as found in Isaiah 7:14, and echoed in Matthew 1:18–25 and Luke 1:27.

Isaiah also spoke of what Jesus would accomplish. He would be a servant and a light to the nations, and the one who opens the eyes of the blind and brings the prisoners out of darkness. He would bring salvation and reconciliation to God for both Gentile and Jew.

In Isaiah 53 we find one of the most poignant passages in all of Scripture referencing Jesus' death.

> Yet He Himself bore our sicknesses,
>> and He carried our pains;
>> but we in turn regarded Him stricken,
>> struck down by God, and afflicted.
> But He was pierced because of our transgressions,
>> crushed because of our iniquities;
>> punishment for our peace was on Him,
>> and we are healed by His wounds.
> We all went astray like sheep;
>> we all have turned to our own way;
>> and the LORD has punished Him
>> for the iniquity of us all.
>
> He was oppressed and afflicted,
>> yet He did not open His mouth.
>> Like a lamb led to the slaughter
>> and like a sheep silent before her shearers,
>> He did not open His mouth.
> He was taken away because of oppression and judgment;
>> and who considered His fate?
>> For He was cut off from the land of the living;
>> He was struck because of my people's rebellion.
> They made His grave with the wicked
>> and with a rich man at His death,
>> although He had done no violence
>> and had not spoken deceitfully.

Yet the LORD was pleased to crush Him severely.

> When You make Him a restitution offering,
>
> He will see His seed, He will prolong His days,
>
> and by His hand, the LORD's pleasure will be accomplished.

He will see it out of His anguish,

> and He will be satisfied with His knowledge.

My righteous Servant will justify many,

> and He will carry their iniquities.

Therefore I will give Him the many as a portion,

> and He will receive the mighty as spoil,
>
> because He submitted Himself to death,
>
> and was counted among the rebels;
>
> yet He bore the sin of many
>
> and interceded for the rebels. (vv. 4–12 HCSB)

In John 17, we find what is referred to as the High Priestly Prayer of Jesus. The final act of the Passion was unfolding. Jesus had washed His disciples' feet as an example of the servanthood that is to characterize believers. He had shared His final meal with them, foretold of His betrayal, given them a new commandment to love one another, explained afresh that He is the only way to the Father, and given them the promise of the Holy Spirit. Now, He turned His face to the Father and spoke to Him as a faithful Son who had fulfilled and would continue to fulfill the prophecies that began with His incarnation. He had been faithful to reveal the Father, to demonstrate the kingdom's power, and He would be faithful to the cross and beyond, to destroy the power of the devil and defeat his work.

With words of triumph that look past the agony of the cross to the resurrection and ascension, to the reward of the glory of God that Jesus wanted His friends to witness, Jesus was calling those things that are not as though they were. His reference to "where I am" spoke of a future reality, soon to be: "Father, I desire that they also, whom you have given me, may be with me where I am, to see my glory that you have given me because you loved me before the foundation of the world" (v. 24 ESV).

When Jesus was captured in the Garden of Gethsemane, He again indicated His understanding of God's plan for Him to embrace the cross. After Peter cut off the ear of the high priest's slave, Jesus said to him, "Put your sword into its sheath; shall I not drink the cup that the Father has given me?" (John 18:11 ESV). Matthew's gospel gives us a fuller version of this incident.

> Then Jesus said to him, "Put your sword back into its place. For all who take the sword will perish by the sword. Do you think that I cannot appeal to my Father, and he will at once send me more than twelve legions of angels? But how then should the Scriptures be fulfilled, that it must be so?" At that hour Jesus said to the crowds, "Have you come out as against a robber, with swords and clubs to capture me? Day after day I sat in the temple teaching, and you did not seize me. But all this has taken place that the Scriptures of the prophets might be fulfilled." Then all the disciples left him and fled. (Matt. 26:52–56 ESV)

Again, at His trial before Pilate, Jesus did not respond like a man who had been trapped by his misguided enthusiasm for the kingdom of God. Rather, He was very much aware of the importance of the hour of His death. John 18:37 captures the moment: "'You are a king, then!' said Pilate. Jesus answered, 'You say that I am a king. In fact, the reason I was born and came into the world is to testify to the truth. Everyone on the side of truth listens to me.'"

Jesus understood that His death was the will of the Father, which was the same as the will of the Son and the Spirit, because He knew all things are in the Father's hands. "'Do you refuse to speak to me?' Pilate said.

'Don't you realize I have power either to free you or to crucify you?' Jesus answered, 'You would have no power over me if it were not given to you from above. Therefore the one who handed me over to you is guilty of a greater sin'" (John 19:10–11).

After He was raised from the dead, we find Jesus teaching His disciples from the Old Testament as He explained the necessity of His crucifixion and resurrection, and the coming of the Spirit to empower them to take the gospel into all the world.

> Then he said to them, "These are my words that I spoke to you while I was still with you, that everything written about me in the Law of Moses and the Prophets and the Psalms must be fulfilled." Then he opened their minds to understand the Scriptures, and said to them, "Thus it is written, that the Christ should suffer and on the third day rise from the dead, and that repentance for the forgiveness of sins should be proclaimed in his name to all nations, beginning from Jerusalem. You are witnesses of these things. And behold, I am sending the promise of my Father upon you. But stay in the city until you are clothed with power from on high." (Luke 24:44–49 ESV)

The witness of the church would be connected to the receiving of the new covenant Spirit through which the kingdom of God would advance as a result of the good news of the kingdom of God being proclaimed by the followers of Jesus that would be backed up by signs and wonders (Acts 1:8; Mark 16:15–18).

In answer to Pilate's question of why Jesus had to die, Scripture says that Jesus died to fulfill Scripture. Jesus, obedient to the Father in all things, continues to fulfill the promises of God to His people as found in Scripture, revealing the glory of God through you and me. The commissioning found in Acts 1:8 and Mark 16:15–18 was the evangelism strategy of the apostle Paul, who testified to this reality near the end of his letter to the church at Rome. Open your heart and take hold of these words and make them your evangelism strategy as you testify to their reality in our world today.

> In Christ Jesus, then, I have reason to be proud of my work for God. For I will not venture to speak of anything except what Christ has accomplished through me to bring the Gentiles to obedience—by word and deed, by the power of signs and wonders, by the power of the Spirit of God—so that from Jerusalem and all the way around to Illyricum I have fulfilled the ministry of the gospel of Christ . . . (Rom. 15:17–19 ESV)

CONCLUSION

Something changed in the earth because of the cross of Jesus Christ. Something that had never been possible before is now possible for every child of God; not just for kings and prophets—but for everyone who believes in the name of Jesus. Sin has been paid for. Salvation has been made free, appropriated by faith and rooted in grace. The new covenant, inaugurated on the cross of Christ, makes it possible for us to be filled with the Holy Spirit.

Jesus has reconciled us to His Father, who loves us so much that within the Trinity of Father, Son, and Holy Spirit, the love of God reached out in and through the life of Jesus to reveal this great and unfathomable love. We are forgiven and reconciled to God. Yet, for you and me to benefit from what has happened, we have to Accept the offer of salvation and reconciliation; Believe on Jesus, trusting Him and Him alone for the basis of our salvation; and Confess or agree with God in acknowledging our sin. Then, we must Commit our life to God. It is these four steps—acceptance, belief, confession, and commitment—that bring us to the place where we are reconciled by grace through faith in Jesus and what He has done for us.

As we stand reconciled, Jesus will Deliver us from death, demons, and damnation, which is the second death, granting us instead eternal life—immortality that is a gift from God, not the natural condition of every soul. God desires to not only count you righteous, but also to make you righteous. He wants to not only justify you but also sanctify you.

There are three big lies the devil likes to tell us to keep us from experiencing the fullness of God's salvation.

Lie #1: You're so good that you can go to heaven because of your goodness; you don't need a savior. You're not bad enough that God would withhold the gift of eternal life.

God's Truth: In the garden, before He went to the cross, Jesus prayed, "If there were any other way, then let the cross be taken from Me." As we know, Jesus went to the cross. Therefore, there is no other way. Otherwise, the Father would be a liar and a very cruel God who just stood by while His beloved Son endured the brutality of the cross.

Lie #2: You're so bad that God won't save you. You've sinned so much that the grace and mercy of the cross have run out for you—the work of the cross just wasn't quite adequate to cover your sin.

God's Truth: The benefits of the cross are available to all who believe on the name of Jesus, having their wills set free to believe by the prevenient grace of God, and the work of the cross is a finished work. God's will is that all would come to repentance.

Lie #3: Put salvation off to some point in the future; you don't need to be saved today, right now. You've got time.

God's Truth: The Bible tells us that no one can come to the Father except through Jesus, and that unless the Spirit of God draws you, you can't come. God has a special opportunity for you— His divine invitation, when He knocks at the door of your heart. It is important that we understand the immeasurable value of that moment, that knock, and not squander our opportunity. The devil wants us to operate under the deception that there is no urgency to the knock of God, until we get to the place where we don't feel Him wooing us any longer.

Two nights before the car accident that changed my life, I was with my friend Joe. "I want to do what you've done, Randy," Joe said. "I respect you. I want to become a good Catholic. When I'm older, when I'm thirty, I'm going to quit doing all this [wild living]." Two days later, Joe, one of my best friends, was seated next to me in the car, was thrown through the windshield, and died. I felt like I had failed him, that I had missed the opportunity to tell him of the urgency of the knock of God for his life. For months afterward, I would go out to the graveyard to deal with my grief. I would sit next to Joe's grave and just say what was in my heart. "Joe," I would say, "I'm so sorry I didn't tell you about Jesus. When it was obvious God was working in your life, I didn't tell you about the gospel. I wish I could go back to that moment and do it over." I wasn't talking to the dead in those moments. I was grieved for my friend.

GOD'S DIVINE INVITATION

It is my hope and prayer that you, having read this far, can embrace the conclusion regarding who Jesus is, what He is, why He came into the world, and why He died, as well as His ongoing ministry. If you have not yet benefited from His person and work, it is my heart's desire that you be enlightened by the Holy Spirit as to who Jesus truly is, and—having been enlightened as to why He had to die—you will want to know the One who loves you and has already died on your behalf to reconcile you to God, His Father. For God loves you so much that within the Trinity of Father, Son, and Holy Spirit, He reached out in and through the life of Jesus to reveal this greatest of all loves.

Through the work of Jesus on the cross you have been forgiven and reconciled to the Father. Yet, for you to benefit from what happened on the cross you have to:

Accept the offer of salvation and reconciliation.

Believe on Jesus, trusting Him and Him alone for the basis of your salvation.

Confess or agree with God in acknowledging you have sinned and are a sinner.

Commit your life to God and be reconciled by grace through faith in Jesus and what He has done for you.

If you do this, He will:

Deliver you from death, demons, and damnation, which is the second death, granting you instead eternal life—immortality that is a gift from God, not the natural condition of every soul.

He wants to not only count you righteous but also make you righteous. He wants to not only justify you but sanctify you.

For those of you who have already been reconciled to God the Father, through Jesus the Son by the power of the Holy Spirit, I hope you will benefit from the other reasons Jesus died, and the other reasons He came into the world, taking upon Himself our nature through the incarnation. May you walk in the new covenant, experiencing the graces of the gifts of the Spirit, enlightened by His wisdom and knowledge, empowered by the filling or baptism of the Holy Spirit, thus enabling you to fulfill God's calling and destiny in and through you.

Something changed in the earth, something that had never been possible before, not just for kings and prophets but for every child of God. Sin has been paid for. Salvation has been made free, appropriated by grace. The new covenant makes it possible for us to be filled with the Holy Spirit. Jesus died so that we could be forgiven and born again. Someone asked me if forgiveness and new birth are the same thing. What we have are two different metaphors. However, if there is no new creation then there has been no real born-again experience of the Holy Spirit.

Many people think they've been born again because they believe in the gospel. People who have had an emotional experience and were water baptized think they are eternally secure and don't need to worry about their salvation. There are those who believe in eternal security and teach that the evidence that you've had a real salvation experience is that you do not fall away, that you persevere until the end. My question to you again is, "No matter how emotional your experience might have been, did it result in you becoming a new creation? Has there been a change in your life? If there has not, are you really born again?"

Remember, if you have been baptized in the Holy Spirit, the evidence will be the changes that take place in you. I didn't know that there was such a possibility. Yet, looking back, I had a wonderful born-again experience. There was a filling by the Holy Spirit that happened to me. However, not everyone's experience is the same; some are more dramatic than others. I had three post-conversion experiences. Two of my experiences of being filled with the Holy Spirit were accompanied by great power that manifested in my physical body accompanied by great emotion.

I ask you now, "Who do you want me to release to you: Jesus or Barabbas? Do you want a savior, a deliverer, a healer, a baptizer who can fill you? Or do you want someone who will steal and destroy and deceive and ruin your life?"

Your choice will ultimately cost you not only your earthly life but your eternal life as well. I believe that in this moment the Holy Spirit is going to do what He is supposed to do—He is going to come and you will feel His presence as if I am writing this just to you and you alone because this message is for you.

The Holy Spirit is going to do a work in you. He is going to draw you to the Father and the Son. His job is to convince you of your sin and your need for righteousness in Christ, and of a judgment to come.

If you are so privileged that right now, while you are reading this, the Holy Spirit is inviting you to accept Christ, then don't throw away the invitation! If the Holy Spirit is drawing you, reach out and take hold of what He offers you. Do it now, because it is only by invitation that you can be drawn to Jesus. No act of your will or decision of your mind can broker this divine invitation. It is a work of God; He must draw you. The Bible says you can't come to the Father except through Jesus, and you can't come to Jesus unless the Spirit draws you. Understand the value of God's divine invitation. If He is knocking at the door of your heart, receive Him!

Perhaps you can identify with something in my story. Perhaps some of you are not yet born again. Perhaps you have lost your first love and begun to backslide. Perhaps you are a hypocrite wearing a mask, pretending to be something you are not. Perhaps you are living a double life. Whatever your situation, may the hound of heaven let you know that He is on your trail. May He set up divine appointments in your life that lead you to the knowledge of Jesus, the living Word, God come in the flesh.

God hates sin because it hurts the people He created and loves. If God is dealing with you right now, convicting you of the need to change how you live and to live for Him, respond to Him. If He is giving you faith to believe in His love for you, faith to believe in His grace to forgive you and empower you to live a better life; don't throw away this opportunity to open the door of your heart to God.

I am giving an invitation to you right now; an invitation to ask God to forgive you of the things you have done that hurt yourself or others; an invitation to ask Jesus into your life, to receive His blessing, and to receive all of the benefits of the cross:

Salvation
Deliverance
Forgiveness
Healing
Filling with the Holy Spirit

I believe the Holy Spirit will knock on the door of your heart right now and convict you of those things you need to deal with, whether it is wearing a mask pretending to be a Christian when you are not or doing things that aren't pleasing to God. Whatever it is, I believe He is speaking to your heart right now in a way that is specific to you. Choose this day whom you will serve. However, don't choose unless His prevenient grace is present—the grace that comes before you choose Him that gives you the faith to believe He will accept you and forgive you.

As you prepare to confess your sins, remember, Jesus is your defense attorney. According to Scripture, your confession places your case in His hands, metaphorically speaking.

If we confess our sins, he is faithful and just and will forgive us our sins and purify us from all unrighteousness. (1 John 1:9)

As far as the east is from the west, so far has he removed our transgressions from us. (Ps. 103:12)

You will cast all our sins into the depths of the sea. (Mic. 7:19 NRSV)

If Jesus is knocking on the door of your heart right now, join me in praying this prayer:

Father, in the name of Jesus, I thank You for awakening me to my need of salvation.

I thank You for convicting me of my sins and that I am a sinner who needs forgiveness.

I thank You for the godly sorrow You have brought into my soul to draw me to Jesus.

I do not ask You to forgive me because of anything good I have done or will do after today.

I am asking You to forgive my sins not on the basis of my self-righteousness, but on the basis of Jesus' righteousness.

I believe You will forgive me because of Jesus' death on the cross for my sins.

Jesus, I thank You for dying for me.

Holy Spirit, I thank You for convicting me and drawing me to Jesus.

Almighty God, hear my confession.

Take a moment to ask God to forgive you of specific sins that have caused you sorrow, regret, or hurt, or perhaps have hurt others. (This is often when people experience tears, but not always.) Whatever God brings to your memory, confess it as sin and ask for forgiveness. Do not rush this moment. When you are done confessing the sins that come to your mind, then you can proceed to the prayer below.

Thank You, Father.

Thank You, Jesus.

Thank You, Holy Spirit.

Thank You for hearing my prayer.

Thank You for forgiving my sins.

Thank You for giving me eternal life.

I commit my life to You. Give me the power of Your Holy Spirit; enable me to live for Your honor and glory.

Fill me with Your Spirit.

Cause Your gifts of the Holy Spirit to flow into my life.

Teach me how to hear from You.

Teach me how to follow the leading of Your Spirit.

In Jesus' name, amen.

So, what should you do now? First, find a good Bible-believing church that welcomes the presence and gifts of the Holy Spirit. Be baptized and become an active part of that church, remembering that you have gifts that God wants to release through you to others in that local body, as well as in and through your life wherever you live and work.

Read your Bible, pray, and meditate on scriptures. Share your faith with others, and reveal God's love and compassion to others. Share this book with others. Study the different chapters, until you can talk about the reasons Jesus died on the cross to others. Become a friend of Jesus for life!

". . . so the Son of Man must be lifted up, that everyone who believes in Him may have eternal life. For God so loved the world that He gave His one and only Son, that everyone who believes in Him shall not perish but have eternal life."

—JOHN 3:14–16 BSB

ACKNOWLEDGMENTS

I want to give special thanks to my daughter Johanna who has encouraged me over the years to finish her favorite sermon of mine on the reasons why Jesus had to die.

To Joel, for your vision to take on this project for Emanate. To Lauren, for your expertise in guiding this book through to completion. To Susan, for your content development and editing throughout this project.

Thanks to Michael White for helping with chapters 12 and 13.

Special thanks to Vicki, for being my administrator extraordinaire and jumping in on this project whenever I needed you.

APPENDIX

Translation History Behind Romans 15:19

I chose the English Standard Version for these verses in Romans because it more faithfully represents the Greek, which does not have the word *preached* in verse 19, which was added by translators. Four of the five sixteenth-century English translations do not include the word *preached*. This indicates that the ESV is not some twenty-first-century novel translation. It was Dr. Jon Ruthven who first made me aware of this. I remember sharing the finding with the pastor of the largest Protestant church in Athens, Greece. He went to his Greek New Testament and was quite amazed to find that I was correct in this observation.

> For I will not venture to speak of anything except what Christ has accomplished through me to bring the Gentiles to obedience—by word and deed, by the power of signs and wonders, by the power of the Spirit of God—so that from Jerusalem and all the way around to Illyricum I have fulfilled the ministry of the gospel of Christ.
>
> —ROMANS 15:18–19 ESV

Tyndale 1526: "For I dare not speake of eny of tho thinges which Christ hath not wrought by me to make the gentyls obedient with

worde and dede in myghty signes and wonders by the power of
the sprete of God: so that from Ierusalem and the costes rounde
aboute vnto Illyricum I have fylled all countres with the gladde
tydynges of Christ."

Miles Coverdale 1535: "For I durst not speake ought, excepte Christ
had wroughte the same by me, to make the Heythen obediet
thorow worde and dede, thorow the power of tokens and wonders, and thorow the power of the sprete of God, so that from
Ierusale, and roude aboute vnto Illyricon, I haue *fylled all with the
Gospell of Christ.*"

The Geneva Bible 1560: "With the power of signes and wonders, by
the power of the Spirit of God: so that from Hierusalem, and
round about vnto Illyricum, I haue *caused to abound the Gospel of
Christ.*"

Bishops Bible 1560: "In myghtie signes and wonders, by the power
of the spirite of God: so that from Hierusalem, and the coastes
rounde about, vnto Illyricum, I haue fullye *preached the Gospell of
Christe.*" (The first to add "preached" in the translation, which is
not in the Greek.)

Douay-Rheims 1582: "By the virtue of signs and wonders, in the
power of the Holy Ghost, so that from Jerusalem round about, as
far as unto Illyricum, I have *replenished the gospel of Christ.*"

The following passages reinforce the importance of power accompa-
nying the preaching of the gospel—not to prove it was correct doctrine
but as part of the good news that the power of the Kingdom of God was
breaking in upon our fallen world. These signs and wonders, healings and
miracles were actually expressions of the gospel itself and were to accompany the words of the gospel. The gospel was not word alone but word
and deed. I also realize that in the context of these verses, sometimes the

power is to strengthen the believers in their difficulties, persecutions, and tribulations, which also points to the fact that the reference is not limited to making us only more moral, but gives us the power to live victoriously in the face of spiritual warfare and the power to work signs and wonders, healing and miracles.

1 Corinthians 2:4–5: "My message and my preaching were not with wise and persuasive words, but with a demonstration of the Spirit's power, so that your faith might not rest on human wisdom, but on God's power."

2 Corinthians 4:7: "But we have this treasure in jars of clay to show that this all-surpassing power is from God and not from us."

2 Corinthians 12:9 (emphasis mine): "But he said to me, 'My grace is sufficient for you, for my power is made perfect in weakness.' Therefore I will boast all the more gladly about my weaknesses, so *that Christ's power may rest on me*."

2 Corinthians 13:4 (emphasis mine): "For to be sure, he was crucified in weakness, yet he lives by God's power. Likewise, we are weak in him, *yet by God's power we will live with him in our dealing with you*."

Ephesians 1:17–20 ESV (emphasis mine): "That the God of our Lord Jesus Christ, the Father of glory, may give you the Spirit of wisdom and of revelation in the knowledge of him, having the eyes of your hearts enlightened, that you may know what is the hope to which he has called you, what are the riches of his glorious inheritance in the saints, and what is the *immeasurable greatness of his power toward us who believe*, according to the working of his great might that he worked in Christ when he raised him from the dead and seated him at his right hand in the heavenly places."

Ephesians 3:16: "I pray that out of his glorious riches he may strengthen you with power through his Spirit in your inner being."

Colossians 1:11: "Being strengthened with all power according to his glorious might so that you may have great endurance and patience."

1 Thessalonians 1:5: "Because our gospel came to you not simply with words but also with power, with the Holy Spirit and with deep conviction. You know how we lived among you for your sake."

2 Thessalonians 1:11 (emphasis mine): "With this in mind, we constantly pray for you, that our God may count you worthy of his calling, and that *by his power he* may bring to fruition your every desire for goodness and your every deed prompted by faith."

REFERENCES FOR FURTHER EXPLORATION

CHAPTER 6: JESUS DIED SO WE COULD BE BAPTIZED *IN*, *WITH*, AND *BY* THE HOLY SPIRIT

Matthew 3:11

Mark 1:8

Luke 3:16

John 1:33

John 3:5–7

Acts 1:4–5

Romans 15:18–19

1 Corinthians 12:13

Ephesians 4:30

Hebrews 4:14; 5:5

Hebrews 9:12

Hebrews 9:15

Hebrews 12:24

CHAPTER 7: JESUS DIED TO BECOME THE MEDIATOR OF THE NEW COVENANT

Matthew 3:11

Mark 1:8

CHAPTER 12: JESUS DIED TO DISPLAY THE JUSTICE AND HOLINESS OF THE TRIUNE GOD

Exodus 13:21

Psalm 51:5

Matthew 12:25

Romans 3:23

CHAPTER 13: JESUS DIED TO DEMONSTRATE THE RIGHTEOUSNESS OF GOD

Luke 9:23

John 14:3–4

2 Timothy 2:4

1 Peter 3:18

CHAPTER 14: JESUS DIED SO THAT WE MIGHT BE RECONCILED TO THE FATHER

John 3:8

Romans 8:13–16

2 Corinthians 5:17

Galatians 5:25

Colossians 1:29

1 Peter 4:6

CHAPTER 15: JESUS DIED TO BECOME
OUR MODEL AND PROPHET

Matthew 4:17

Matthew 16:24–26

Matthew 25

John 14:6

John 14:12–14

Acts 3:22

Acts 7:37

1 Corinthians 4:16

2 Corinthians 5:18–20

Colossians 2:15

Hebrews 4:16–18

Revelation 5:5–6

NOTES

Introduction

1. Conrad Hackett and David McClendon, "Christians Remain World's Largest Group, but They Are Declining in Europe," Pew Research Center, Apr. 5, 2017, https://www.pewresearch.org/fact-tank/2017/04/05/christians-remain-worlds -largest-religious-group-but-they-are-declining-in-europe/.

2. Craig S. Keener, *The IVP Bible Background Commentary, New Testament*, Ebook, Second Edition (Downers Grove, IL: InterVarsity Press, 2014).

3. Debbie McDaniel, "50 Names and Titles of Jesus: Who the Bible Says Christ Is," Dec. 1, 2016, www.Crosswalk.com, Salem Media Group, https://www.crosswalk .com/blogs/debbie-mcdaniel/50-names-of-jesus-who-the-bible-says-christ-is.html.

Chapter 1: Jesus Died to Destroy Captivity

1. Ramsay MacMullen, *Christianizing the Roman Empire AD 100–400* (New Haven, CT: Yale University Press, 1984).

2. Randy Clark, *The Biblical Guidebook to Deliverance* (Lake Mary, FL: Charisma Media, 2015), xvi-xvii, xxviii.

Chapter 2: Jesus Died to Release the Power and Authority to Heal

1. James Strong, *Strong's Exhaustive Concordance of the Bible* (Abingdon Press, 1890), 7495.

Chapter 3: Jesus Died to Destroy Death

1. This story can also be found on CBN: www1.cbn.com/content/dr-chauncey -crandall-raising-dead.

Chapter 5: Jesus Died So That He Might Ransom People

1. Gustaf Aulén, *Christus Victor: An Historical Study of the Three Main Types of the Idea of Atonement* (Eugene, OR: Wipf & Stock Publishers, 2003).

2. Gregory Boyd, *God at War* (Downers Grove, IL: IVP Academic, 1997), 255–9.

3. Randy Clark, *Baptized in the Spirit: God's Presence Resting upon You with Power* (Shippensburg, PA: Destiny Image Publishers, Inc., 2017), 132.

4. *Nicene and Post-Nicene Fathers*, series 2, vol. 4, ed. Philip Schaff and Henry Wace, trans. R. Payne-Smith (Buffalo, NY: Christian Literature Publishing Co., 1892). Revised and edited for New Advent by Kevin Knight, http://www.newadvent.org /fathers/2806004.htm.

5. This Greek word is translated "sanctification" thirty-three times and "holiness" ten times in my Bible software program, Accordance.

Chapter 6: Jesus Died So We Could Be Baptized in, with, and by the Holy Spirit

1. J. D. Lightfoot, *The Whole Works of Rev. John Lightfoot, D.D.*, Volume XII, ed. John Rogers Pitman (London: J. F. Dove, 1823), 3874.

2. I capitalize *Charismatic* as I do *Pentecostal* because in other countries like Mexico, Argentina, and Brazil, there are denominations with the name Charismatic.

3. Randy Clark, *Baptized in the Spirit: God's Presence Resting upon You with Power*; *There Is More: Reclaiming the Power of Impartation*; *Changed in a Moment*; *God Can Use Little Ole Me*; *Lighting Fires*.

Chapter 7: Jesus Died to Become the Mediator of the New Covenant

1. Strong, 3316.

2. Craig S. Keener, *The IVP Bible Background Commentary New Testament*, 2nd ed. (Downers Grove, IL: InterVarsity Press, 2014), 654; location 21078 Kindle version.

3. William Whitaker (1548–1595): Gifted Cambridge Puritan theologian. Author of *Disputations on Holy Scripture* and a contributor to the Lambeth Articles. Born in Holme, Lancashire. Taken from *Puritan Sermons 1659–1689, The Morning Exercises at Cripplegate*, vol. 5, sermon 13.

4. Whitaker, *Puritan Sermons*.

5. Randy Clark, *Baptized in the Spirit: God's Presence Resting Upon You with Power* (Shippensburg, PA: Destiny Image Publishers, Inc, 2017).

Chapter 8: Jesus Died to Become Our Great High Priest

1. Frank Stagg, *New Testament Theology* (Nashville, TN: Broadman Press, 1962), 68–9.

2. Dale Moody, *The Word of Truth: A Summary of the Christian Doctrine Based upon Biblical Revelation* (Grand Rapids, MI: Eerdmans Publishing Company, 1981), 375–7.

3. Moody, 375–7.

4. Mary Healy, *Catholic Commentary on Sacred Scripture, Hebrews* (Grand Rapids, MI: Baker Academic, 2016), 101–2.

Chapter 9: Jesus Died So That We Might Be Forgiven

1. Nicky Cruz, *Run, Baby, Run* (Newberry, FL: Bridge-Logos Publishers, 1968).

2. David Wilkerson with John and Elizabeth Sherrill, *The Cross and the Switchblade* (New York: Random House, 1963).

Chapter 10: Jesus Died So That We May Have Eternal Life

1. Michael McClymond, *The Devil's Redemption: A New History and Interpretation of Christian Universalism* (Grand Rapids: Baker Academic, 2018).

Chapter 12: Jesus Died to Display the Justice and Holiness of the Triune God

1. E. W. Kenyon and R. A. Kenyon, *The Blood Covenant* (Lynnwood, WA: Kenyon's Gospel Publishing Society, 1995), 9.

Chapter 13: Jesus Died to Demonstrate the Righteousness of God

1. Moody, 328.
2. Moody, 326.
3. Under the Old Testament dispensation, the only three categories of people who could hear from God were prophets, priests, and kings.
4. Strong, G38.

Chapter 14: Jesus Died So That We Might Be Reconciled to the Father

1. Moody, 329–30. Quoting James Denny, *The Death of Christ*, 2nd ed. (New York: A. C. Armstrong and Son, 1903), 143ff.
2. Moody, 330, 331.

Chapter 15: Jesus Died to Become Our Model and Prophet

1. Jon Ruthven, *On the Cessation of the Charismata* (Tulsa, OK: Word & Spirit Press, 1993, 2011).
2. Philip Schaff, *A Select Library of the Nicene and Post-Nicene Fathers of the Christian Church*, series 2, vol. 2 (Grand Rapids, MI: William B. Eerdmans Publishing Company, 1983), 345.
3. Mark Galli, Ted Olsen, *131 Christians Everyone Should Know* (Nashville, TN: Holman Reference, 2000), 305.
4. Walter Wink, *The Powers That Be: Theology for a New Millennium* (New York: Doubleday Pub., 1998). Wink's book is helplful in understanding how the demonic influences corporations, governments, and through ideologies, but it is weak in that it doesn't agree with the reality of personal demons who can demonize people. *The Twilight Labrynth*, by George Otis Jr., deals with the impact of the powers over regions or areas and would be helpful to the students who read Wink to gain a broader perspective and vice versa. A few of Peter Wagner's books on this subject would also be helpful.

Chapter 16: Jesus Died to Fulfill God's Original Plan

1. Taken from the author's unpublished March 29 entry for NewSong Church's Passion Week Devotional.
2. Joachim Jeremias, *Jerusalem in the Time of Jesus* (Philadelphia, PA: Fortress Press, 1969), 84.

ABOUT THE AUTHOR

Randy Clark is best known for helping to spark the movement of God now affectionately labeled "the Toronto Blessing." In the years since, his influence has grown as an international speaker. He continues, with great tenacity, to demonstrate the Lord's power to heal the sick. Randy received his Master of Divinity from The Southern Baptist Theological Seminary and his Doctor of Ministry and Doctor of Divinity from United Theological Seminary (Dayton, Ohio). He has written more than forty books, and his message is simple: "God wants to use you." The most important aspect of his calling to ministry is the way God uses him for impartation.

John Wimber heard God speak audibly the first two times he met Randy, telling John that Randy would one day go around the world laying his hands on pastors and leaders for the impartation and activation of the gifts of the Holy Spirit. In January 1994, in the early days of the outpouring of the Spirit in Toronto, John called Randy and told him that what God had shown him about Randy a decade earlier was beginning now. It has continued ever since. Randy has the unique ability to minister to many denominations and apostolic networks. These have included Roman Catholics, Messianic Jews, Methodists, Reformed, Lutheran, many Pentecostal and Charismatic congregations, and the largest Baptist churches in Argentina, Brazil, and South Africa. He has also taken several thousand people with him on international ministry teams. Bill Johnson says the fastest way to increase in the supernatural is to accompany Randy on an international trip. Randy has traveled to more than fifty-four countries, including 116 trips to Brazil through 2019, and continues to travel extensively to see that God's mandate on his life is fulfilled.

Randy and his wife, DeAnne, reside in Mechanicsburg, Pennsylvania. They have four adult children, all married, and eight grandchildren. For more information about Randy Clark, his ministry, and his resource materials, visit www.GlobalAwakening.com. To invite Dr. Randy Clark to minister, contact his personal assistant, Vicki@globalawakening.com. For more information about Global Awakening Theological Seminary, visit https://Seminary.FamilyofFaith.edu.